He hath made every thing beautiful.

(Ecclesiastes 3:11.)

A SEARCH FOR SENSI-TIVITY & SPIRIT

RICHARD L. GUNN

Deseret Book Company
Salt Lake City, Utah
1981

© 1981 Deseret Book Company
All rights reserved
Printed in the United States of America

First printing March 1981

Library of Congress Cataloging in Publication Data

Gunn, Richard L 1918-
  A search for sensitivity and spirit.

  Bibliography: p.
  Includes index.
  1. Christian life—Mormon authors.   2. Christianity
and the arts.   3. Gunn, Richard L., 1918-   I. Title.
BX8656. G86   248.4'8933   80-26646
ISBN 0-87747-851-1

To Jeanne,

who has shared my search,

and to my children —
Kaye, Elizabeth, Rick,
Tom, Becky, and Candy —
who have been great
teachers in the search
as well as treasures.

Contents

Foreword by Jeffrey R. Holland   ix

Acknowledgments   xi

Introduction   xiii

Part I   The Search Between Brambles and Buttercups

1   An Awesome Discovery   3

2   Pitfalls or Pedestals   8

3   The Struggle for Spiritual Strength   21

Part II   Home Is More than a Hat Hanger

4   Key Words for Family Fixing   33

5   Inside the Front Door   42

6   In Front of the Outside Door   59

Part III   "If Men Were Fish the Last Thing They'd Discover Would Be Water"

7   The Ooohs and Ouches of Community Sensitivity   69

8   Hot Bread and Warm Neighbors   79

9   "His Taste Is All in His Mouth"   92

Part IV   The House of Highest Spirit

10   Symbols and Spiritual Security   103

11   Holes in Our Holiness   113

12   More Than a Steeple   123

Part V   Searching below the Skin of Beauty

13   Exploring a Pioneer Masterpiece   133

14   A Part of the Heart of Art   146
15   Seeing with Aesthetic Vision   163

Part VI The Search for Spiritual and Sensitive Powers
16   Spiritual Energy   181
17   Exploring Sensitive Thought   186
18   Stretching Sensitivity's Stride   196
Postscript   203
Bibliography   205
Index   211

Foreword

Several years ago the Commissioner's Research Fellowship was created within the Church Educational System to stimulate research and writing by Latter-day Saint scholars on topics of particular (and often unique) value to the Latter-day Saint community. The recipient of that fellowship in 1975 was Dr. Richard L. Gunn, professor of art and design at Brigham Young University. This book is the product of that work.

I suppose it is safe to suggest that *A Search for Sensitivity and Spirit* is the kind of book that probably could not have been written except for the encouragement of such a grant for just such a purpose. It certainly is not an ordinary book. That is not so surprising, however, when the reader notes that it is the ordinary in life that is here being shaken up and sifted and stared at under new light. Furthermore, the book does not follow any of the commercial rules for success. To some it may seem a strange undertaking for a publishing firm like Deseret Book Company. To that I can only say it is the finest kind of compliment to Lowell M. Durham, Jr., and his associates that they were not only interested in but wholeheartedly supportive of this project from the beginning. The publication of this book indicates a certain kind of "spirit and sensitivity" on their part, and I commend them for it.

I have suggested what the book is *not*. What it *is* is an adventure into the spirit of things—especially into the human spirit—as we wake and walk and talk and live. It deals, among other things, with children and with nature and with art. It reveals to us the great impact that creativity and sensitivity and wonder can have on our religious life. It is, above all, a religious book, and you will enjoy it in a spiritual way.

And who, you ask, is Richard Gunn? Well, he is the man for whom the original meaning of "enthusiasm" (divine zeal) must have been intended. Talking a mile a minute in class (roughly 1.6

kilometers a minute when he is dashing through Europe on his now-legendary tours) Dick has for some thirty-three years brought both spirit and sensitivity—enthusiasm—to his teaching of art, art history, and design. He has opened the eyes of thousands of students to a world of beauty and grace. Of almost no other man I know could Shakespeare's encouragement be quite so applicable: Dick does find "tongues in trees, books in the running brooks, sermons in stones, and good in every thing."

This book will help the rest of us do the same.

JEFFREY R. HOLLAND
President, Brigham Young University

Acknowledgments

I wish to express my great appreciation for the support of the Church Commissioners of Education, Elder Neal A. Maxwell and Elder Jeffrey Holland; to Laura Bagshaw for her hours at the typewriter, and all others who were guideposts in the search.

Introduction

Spirit, to me, is the most important word in the English language. In every part of our lives and our environment we search for spirit: from a temporary burst of team spirit on the athletic field to the eternal perspective of the Holy Spirit.

Spirit is the essential quality of a home, a community, an individual human being, a work of art. Military leaders emphasize the importance of an esprit de corps. Spirit is the heart of the Church, and most prayers petition God's "Spirit to be with us." There are various levels and dimensions of spirit, and I believe the search for spiritual elements on one level can open vision for understanding on other levels, if we care to nudge the search.

Anyone who has discovered spiritual treasures on any level cannot help feeling a new glow within. This glow extends to the football player leaping wildly in the end zone with the winning touchdown as well as to the congregation enjoying the velvet quietness of a spiritual testimony meeting.

"Where there is no vision, the people perish," warn the scriptures. (Proverbs 29:18.) Vision must surely be born of a sensitivity for spiritual things. A prophet is sensitive to the divine; an artist is sensitive to the aesthetic; a family should be sensitive to "togetherness." If we accept only a part of a prophet's vision, we eventually miss a higher level of joy. If we are content to have mediocre art in our homes or churches, we miss a higher level of joy, and sensitive visitors may inwardly smile at our level of taste. If we give half-hearted love to our families, we leave stumbling blocks to our children's potentials.

The vision we can gain in a search for sensitivity and spirit can reveal the highest concepts of joy. Conversely, perhaps the greatest tragedies of our own making come from our neglect of sensitive things.

It seems strange that so many shrug off the quest for spiritual sensitivity. Noah gathered only eight persons from the whole world; a multitude demanded the life of Jesus. Many artists who were ignored throughout their lives while they starved in their attic studios were discovered and lauded in another century. A juvenile judge often wishes that a child or a parent bound in misunderstandings had eyes to see, ears to hear, and a heart to feel.

John the apostle saw a man from Nazareth as the Son of God; the Nazarenes saw him only as a neighbor; a man without any spiritual sensitivity saw him as the devil. Jesus saw Peter as the key leader in the kingdom; those without His sensitivity saw only a fisherman. Peter saw the principal of revelation as a great beacon; those near him saw only a rock of a man. Michelangelo saw within a rock a deliverer, David; his fellow sculptors saw only a stone. Watts had the vision of a condenser for a more effective steam engine to change the world; others saw only a puffing kettle.

Are the scriptures only for the peoples of the past who were urged if they had eyes, to see, or ears, to hear? What are the risks of spiritual apathy?

We may not aspire to be prophets or great creators of scientific marvels or masterpieces of art, but the principles are the same for our families and for us individually. A rock in a field may be an irritant to plow around to a farm laborer, but it could be the shape of a design delight to sensitive sight. In any stream of life we live either by design or by happenstance. If life itself is only an accident, then there is no hope; if there is no hope, the people perish, the prophet declares. But he also says that if we have the sensitivity to see, we will have celestial exaltation.

One of my good friends owes his physical life to penicillin. Fleming's brilliant discovery came just in time. Many people before Fleming had seen the penicillium mold on bread or old lemons. Fleming's keener vision was no accident. I am not easily persuaded that any of man's greatest achievements come by chance alone; they are the products of sensitive people who are vitalized by an animating spirit.

Another friend lost his spiritual life to an idea. The day he discovered this idea there was no one sensitive enough to his spiritual needs to inject a better idea. A spiritual leader cannot be everywhere present; each of us has a responsibility to our neighbor—not for scientific marvels, but to be sufficiently sensitive. At this very hour some child's life may depend on some parent's, grandparent's, or baby-sitter's sensitivity to adapt to a crisis.

I feel strongly that the search for sensitivity and spirit is no frill adventure. I think it is the greatest search of our lives, and I hope that something in these pages will prompt others to use their talents and vision in lifting others to higher spiritual lives. I hope that young parents will weave these threads with others into the fabric of their family nights and their children's lives. I hope that young seminary students will explore some of these ideas in their classes.

There is no broad freeway in the search for sensitivity and spirit. Each of us must search unique paths, but there are many places we can walk together. Come join the search for sensitive treasures with the spirit of a child searching a pirate's cove.

The last words that Elder A. Theodore Tuttle heard from President David O. McKay were, "The things of the spirit are real. Take time to meditate." These are indeed valuable words to ponder as we begin our search for sensitivity and spirit.

Part I
The Search Between Brambles
and Buttercups

1
An Awesome Discovery

*The search for sensitivity and spirit
may require a personal exploration where
no road maps have been charted.
Skeptical searchers may suddenly meet a
wide crossroad and walk to an assurance
of an expanding destiny. Confident
searchers may delight in exploring
small winding paths or ask to walk with
a child for a new understanding of life.
But anyone willing to search for sensitive
and spiritual destinations must surely
discover rich treasures, including the
serendipitous excitement of unexpected
rewards tucked into every path.*

One of the most awesome experiences of my life was when I
witnessed the birth of spirit in men who were hollow.

It began with a young soldier who had been wounded in World War II and sent to Bushnell General Military Hospital in Utah. Paralyzed from the chest down, he was straining to move with the aid of a rolling contraption that reminded me of a small jungle gym on wheels. As he worked his way down the hall with great effort, I found myself standing aside to watch his laborious struggle.

The deep pity I felt for him suddenly turned to a gasp, for as he turned the corner a caster caught, his little cage toppled, and he crashed to the floor. Almost instinctively I leaped to rescue him, but as I stooped down, I saw his eyes focus on my feet. Slowly his head lifted as his eyes moved up my legs. I could sense his mind broadcasting the eternal question: "Why me? Why should you be able to walk, play football, go to a dance, climb a mountain, make a living? Why should I be left a nothing? Why should we have wars?"

When his face turned upward enough for me to see his full expression, a shudder ran through me. It was as though someone had thrown acid into his face; that face did not bear a physical disfigurement, but it had bitter, wrenching features, with steel lines etched hard around his mouth, and glazed eyes.

The impression of this young man's face made such an impact on me that I could not move for a few moments. Almost like a coward I retreated back the way I had come for another route to the hospital office.

Frustration, resignation, and despair were visiting at every bedside at that hospital. Through the doorway of one room I saw an attractive young nurse lift a patient's two distorted hands and, with all the encouragement she could muster, plead with him to try again the simple task of pushing a large needle through a matching hole. His hands, twisted by the flames of battle, could not respond. When the needle again missed the mark, his body went limp, and what was left of his spirits sagged with the falling prong.

"I can't, I can't," he cried.

"You must, you must," was her soothing reply. With tender

coaxing the needle was replaced in his mutilated hands. His repeated tries ended repeatedly in failure.

Each door along the hall framed a new tragedy. Each bed held a hollow man without spirit.

To see so many young men at the prime of their lives ripped from their physical prowess was distressing enough, but to witness the decimation of their spirits was frightening. I do not know how long I stood numbed, watching these scenes, until I was brought back to reality with a question from a hospital attendant.

"Mr. Gunn? We've been looking for you. Would you mind if we postponed our interview until after the assembly? We have a special guest here to speak to the patients—Helen Keller. How would you like to meet her?"

Helen Keller! My own spirits grabbed an express elevator out of my gloomy contemplations. Helen Keller had long been one of my greatest inspirations. I took a giant step in appreciation when I first read the pages of her autobiography. Seldom has water run over my hand without causing me to think of Miss Keller's first communication with her teacher, Anne Sullivan, at the water pump. Her sightless eyes had helped to open my eyes; her deaf ears had helped me to hear; her sensitivity had splashed over me.

With the introduction, Miss Keller held out her hand to me and I grasped it eagerly. As she gave me a firm squeeze, my mind envisioned the water that had flowed over this very hand at that water pump for her birth of sensitivity, and then I marveled at the perceptive brilliance she had achieved through these same fingertips. In my grasp I felt more than bone, sinew, and skin; I felt a magnificently beautiful and tender spirit.

Her voice was not easy to understand. She had never heard a sound. She had never seen a mouth form a word. My comments were translated as her companion's fingers tapped out the words I used.

As we talked, a hospital attendant helped a young soldier to our side. Knowing about my background in art, he had brought me a sculptured head that he had created in clay. He asked Miss Keller if she would like to see it; then, realizing that he had used the word *see*, he looked distressed. Miss Keller's companion quickly tapped out the request, and the great lady smiled warmly and stretched out her hands to "see" the head.

I was transfixed with the obvious enjoyment Helen Keller experienced in exploring the clay with her fingertips. Each finger was almost like a sensitive dancer caught up in a moving piece of music. The room became so quiet around this inspirational woman that a beautiful spirit swept through, leaving a tranquillity too soft to echo. The silence was finally broken as she said, "Oh, it is so beautiful! You are an artist!"

Each of us in that small circle had learned in a moment the value of a lifetime search for an appreciation of aesthetic beauty, and the role that such appreciation plays in building a sensitive person.

Meanwhile, the room had filled with patients gathered for the assembly. The administrators generously allowed me to sit near Miss Keller. What she did not see, but what I am sure she felt through spirit, was the tragic sight assembled before us. Some soldiers were in wheelchairs, some in rolling beds, some on crutches, some in cages—a mangled humanity. I looked at the famous guest to assess her reactions. The slant of her eyebrows quickly told me that she had sensed the stark despair and the bitter feelings of the men.

Then came the miracle that is still so clear in my memory that it could have been yesterday rather than more than three decades ago. As this remarkable woman reached out with her words and her radiant being to sculpt new faces on these men, the hard glint in their eyes softened, their faces started to glow, and the bitter lines melted, reflecting the rebirth of spirit. I was so involved with the miracle taking place before my eyes that I lost touch with Miss Keller's words. To this day I cannot recall specifically what she said, but I will never forget her role as a master creator reaching out, figuratively, with her seeing hands not only to resculpture the faces of about forty men, but also to create human spirit.

There seemed no question when the soldiers later left the room that they carried a spirit of determination to do something with their lives. I am convinced that since that memorable experience, many of those soldiers have accomplished more significantly than if they had returned from the war physically whole. Helen Keller not only gave them new spirits; she made them uncommon men.

Whether we exist in the spiritual basement I first found at Bushnell Hospital or on the spiritual heights that I felt when I left, I know that we do live by the spirit. The things that warm our inner being are measured on a kind of spiritual thermometer. What is most important in art or religion may also be best measured on a kind of spiritual thermometer.

2
Pitfalls or Pedestals

*A search for sensitivity and spirit
may start in an exploration of our own
sensitive stirrings, of the family, of
our social institutions, of history, of the
arts, of religious thought, of almost
any facet of life. I should like to start
with the artworks of children, that offer
immediate discoveries.*

Our youngest son, Tommy, came home one afternoon from
kindergarten with a picture he had drawn in class that most of
us would call a scribble. It looked something like this:

When I asked him about it he brightened up and immediately launched into an excited discussion of his picture of a

turkey. He showed me where the bright colors were in the tail, and he told me how the turkey said "Gobble, gobble, gobble."

I was delighted with his response. It revealed to me several things Tommy had enjoyed, and as Tommy noticed my genuine delight, he was lifted again. I pinned the picture on the wall, another lifter.

These few recognitions were enough to prime the new artist; Tommy returned from school the next day with a half-inch stack of turkey drawings! I don't know how the math and reading came out that day, but I could tell it had been a day of excitement. I pinned more pictures on the walls, and Tommy looked at the exhibit and glowed.

Then Tommy went to Sunday School. As a reward for the children's attention to the lesson, the teacher let them color. She had prepared her lesson with dedication, and had included some duplicated drawings of Thanksgiving turkeys for the children to color in.

When Tommy came home with another picture for his turkey collection, with only half a glance I knew the picture was mostly the teacher's. He had not created the turkey; he had only gone through the mechanical motions of filling in the shapes. I could not praise such work; sincerity is essential, and children quickly recognize a phony. Nor did I want to chop Tommy down with a truthful answer about this turkey just at the moment he had discovered art.

I had taken Tommy's other pictures over to the university to show a class and had pinned them to the wall in two rows; however, I needed one more picture to complete the display. Catching him before he had a chance to present me the new drawing, I told him of my exhibit at school and of my need for one more drawing like the ones he had done at school to complete the set. I quickly brought out the crayons and paper and offered him a chair.

He sat in thought for a minute, looked at me out of the corner of his eye, and then stared at the blank paper for another minute. Three minutes passed by, then four. After five minutes without the crayon touching the paper I ventured a question: "What's the matter, Tommy?" Over all the years I have never forgotten his answer: "Daddy, turkeys are too hard to draw."

Who told the creator of a half-inch stack of turkeys that turkeys are too hard to draw? What was the difference in the way Tommy was that Sunday and the way he had been a few days ago at school? Part of the answer was that at school Tommy had made many lines, and each line in each scribbled drawing had meant *turkey*. But when he filled in the coloring-book turkey, each line meant only *fill-in*. His scribbling had a spirit, a soul. The coloring book was a corpse.

To me, Tommy's scribble reflected both the spirit of the artist in the act of creating and the spirit of the turkey that was pecking for his food. The coloring book illustrator had already drawn the turkey, and Tommy was not participating with any empathy to the fowl or its spirit. The teacher had also declared her idea of the turkey, and Tommy with his own ideas did not find a synthesis. He had learned that he could not draw turkeys the way teachers draw turkeys, so his confidence was shaken.

While I was stewing over this turn of events, Tommy went off to Primary. Back he came with another Thanksgiving turkey. His eyes were bright; he had captured something. His picture looked something like this:

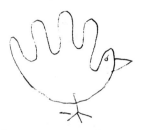

In response to that great question used to help children with their art, "Tell me about your picture," he said, "If you put your hand on a piece of paper and trace around it, all you need to do is add the legs and beak and it makes a turkey." Tommy had regained his confidence—but he had lost his independence. He could meet the task the teacher had given with the formula she had presented, but there was a big price to pay.

Imagine a group of children in a schoolroom happily interrupted by a tail-wagging puppy. After the initial enthusiasm calms down a bit, the teacher might encourage the children to draw the puppy. If they have been through coloring-book or formula-teaching art, probably ninety-nine times out of a hundred they will say, "How do you draw a dog?"

When Tommy scribbled his turkey at school, he didn't ask that question. Assembling his feelings and his knowledge about a turkey, he made a direct body-and-spirit response in lines to communicate his ideas.

After coloring books or other stereotyping experiences, children will usually wait for someone to tell them what to do. They may need to know the trick: "Do you trace around your foot to draw a puppy?" They come to believe that art is a matter of tricks, but tricks seldom reach high enough to touch the levels of spirit that nourish art or children.

What do you do in a turkey dilemma?

One approach is to *strengthen the child's experience* with the object he wants to draw. A turkey ranch in a neighboring town was the target for us, and I loaded Tommy and the other children into the car and we took off. All the turkeys watched us park the car, and as we walked to the fence they strutted over for a closer look.

I had never visited a turkey ranch, and my surprise at the friendly movement of the turkeys prompted me to say, "Hello, girls." I was even more surprised than the children when the turkeys gobbled a very enthusiastic response. Not to be outdone, I gobbled right back at them. The children clapped their hands and cried, "Daddy, can you talk turkey talk?"

That broke the ice with both my children and their feathered friends, and we had a fun experience together. We walked along the fence, and the turkeys trotted right after us. We walked back, and back came the birds. The children were delighted with the parade. Their bright eyes followed pointing fingers to fanning tails, pecking beaks, scratching claws.

The children all started talking to their mother at once when we returned home. Over the chatter I called, "Hold it, hold it, she can't hear you when you all talk at once. Why don't you draw a picture of the turkeys for your mother instead?" Sparkling faces circled the table as we distributed paper and crayons. The crayons had no time to rest between reachings. Spirits splashed. An instant art exhibit was then produced as the children lined up, pictures clutched to chests under their chins. Under Tommy's chin was a drawing similar to the turkeys he had drawn at school, but with a vigorous red addition under the turkey's beak.

This picture was a mystery: I couldn't understand why he had drawn the red beard of a size that endangered the turkey's balance. When I asked about his picture, he explained that the turkey had a funny red thing that hung by his chin. Suddenly I did understand; I could remember wondering myself about that strange bit of turkey anatomy.

My reactivated artist must have been fascinated by the turkey's red wattle as he studied the birds. The wattle in the coloring book had meant nothing to him; his mind in neutral, he had learned nothing positive from the coloring-book experience, and the wattle had received no special attention. But at the turkey ranch he was a student, quickened with experience, perceptually probing all the details. With obvious interest he studied the wattle as it plopped about while the turkey pecked in the dust. That interest and study were openly revealed by the way Tommy magnified the wattle in his drawing.

Parents can learn much about their children's interests and learning by studying their drawings. I knew through Tommy's drawing that he had been involved in a seeing and learning experience, a search for sensitivity.

Since that day I have been a foe of coloring books. I have not torn coloring books into shreds when I have found them at home; that's a tactic that makes children dependent in another direction. Rather, I have said to my children, "Oh, anyone can do coloring books. What I like is when you do your *own* drawing. I like it best when you do it *your* way." When parents like it *his* way, the child also receives the message that he is loved.

Stereotyped activities of any kind not only stomp on the child's spirit, but, more importantly, they may also cause the child to lose confidence in himself. How often we hear people say, "I can't draw!" Who told them so? It is true that everyone does not need to draw and that there are many expressive creative activities besides art, but the same principles hold true in all of these activities. In some cultures everyone is expected to carve his own decoration on the eaves of his house or to paint his own designs on his canoe — and everyone does.

Each person has an artist inside, but stereotyped art activities strangle the art spirit.

I once went to school with one of my daughters to see her class's Christmas pictures. The closer we came to her schoolroom the more excited she became. "There's my Santa Claus!" she started to say as the door swung wide. Then her smile faded as she looked at many Santas that had been cut from the teacher's patterns and pasted together into rows and rows of look-alikes. As she finally confessed that she didn't know which Santa was hers, she salvaged a bit of recognition relief: "Well, that one with the mouth pasted upside down is Jimmy's." Jimmy became my hero, even if it was an accident.

A row of look-alike Santas tells nothing of the child's spirit or of his experience. We have closed the gate to the search for sensitivity and spirit if Santas, turkeys, or trees all look the same. Children with a common experience may draw in similar ways as they influence each other, but where individuality shows, the child is learning. When we recognize this individuality as adults, we too are learning.

The way children draw changes with how they see, what they have experienced, and the level of their spiritual vitality. Study how a child draws trees. Usually a child's first contact with a tree is the trunk. The top of the tree is an unidentifiable thing that is way up above him. From his experience, then, he may at first draw a tree with a massive trunk and an unidentifiable top. (Figure A.) As he grows older and climbs into a tree,

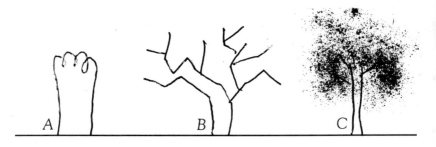

his concept of a tree will change. He may be forming impressions of a tree with branches that shoot out at sharp angles; he may perhaps even have noticed hard twigs scratching or poking him. If this natural jungle gym absorbs his perceptions, he may never see the leaves; his picture of the angled branches will then be true to what he has experienced. (Figure B.)

A person's *experience* with an object is more important than the object itself. Experience touches inner spirit. A picture of a light socket in an advertisement will have no meaning at all to a child until he puts his finger into a socket while the electricity is connected. His concept (or picture) of a light socket before a shocking experience would be quite different from the one after, and obviously the drawing after the shock would be more vital. What the artist brings to his picture is a significant part of his artistic expression.

But if a teacher or parent shows a child how to draw a tree with a tricky technique such as a sponge lightly dipped in paint to magically print out a realistic appearance of leaves (Figure C), the child will likely be impressed with the *how to* of the experience, and will fail to draw upon the *spirit* of the experience. Unfortunately, parents will praise these more life-like trees, and the child is thus encouraged to find new tricks in order to earn praise. Along with the child's loss of "tree spirit" is an even more important loss—creativity. The search for sensitivity ends in a blind alley.

A news release about a paint-by-number kit openly stated: "Personalized Portrait Kit. If the amateur fills in all the areas with similarly numbered paints, he will produce a realistic portrait free from the unorthodox colors and contours that characterize most amateur work, and will do so without any wear and tear on his imagination. . . . After an eye-straining four hours, thirty-three children succeeded in converting their canvases into almost identical replicas. . . ."

It's no wonder that the sensitive and creative artist tucked inside each person is flattened palette-thin with so many spirit-draining techniques. For over thirty years I have taught young children, junior and senior high school students, university students, and grandparents. I testify that something happens along time's trail that slowly robs an average person of some or all of the sensitive stirrings within him. The search for sensitivity and spirit is often difficult.

A visit to Virginia Tanner's dance class for children was a most memorable experience in finding sensitivity and spirit. Miss Tanner's school had a reputation for molding children into fine dancers. Actually, I think she was less interested in making the children superior dancers than in helping them become more sensitive persons. A superior dancer is less a person of technique than a person of spirit. The Tanner school taught the child to be a sensitive personality first, and then he could be a fine dancer or a performer in any of many other fields.

A visit to Miss Tanner's classroom was an adventure in sensitivity. We watched her drop a silver dollar to the floor. The children watched the coin fall, and they listened to it quiver to quiet. Dropping it again, the teacher helped the children watch the coin more perceptively. Eventually their perceptions were translated into dance form, and the children fell to the dance floor as though they were silver dollars quivering and shimmering on the floor. Later they fell to the floor as feathers.

In front of an audience, children are not silver dollars; in the classroom Miss Tanner was teaching awareness and sensitivity. With such sense-sharpening these children could walk along an autumn path as the leaves fall and, where many of us would see a falling leaf only as a clue that winter is about to arrive, these dancers might pause to study an autumn leaf in flight, to notice it sliding from one layer of air to another, dipping and coasting in one last ballet on the tiptoes of the stem. Some of these children might even move their bodies to echo the leaf's rhythm. In front of an audience such children dance with sensitive depth.

Parents who have not been members of a Tanner dance class and who have been flooded instead with coloring books must not let this be cause to give up the search for sensitivity and spirit. No one is completely sense-lost. Surely every adult remembers kicking through the dry leaves or jumping into Dad's raked pile; it was a moment of sensitive growth when we kicked dry leaves and listened. Our childhoods were not lived in vacuums. We may not be a Miss Tanner, but as parents, we are the most important teachers of our children. The greater our search for sensitivity, the greater will be the growth of any children we contact, not merely our own.

With the spirit of Virginia Tanner guiding me, I visited a high school art class. I heard a groan of failure, then the sound of paper being crumpled. A wad flew through the air headed for the wastebasket. My attempt to guide it into the basket failed, so I bent over to pick it up for more direct targeting. With a

mental nudge from Miss Tanner I decided instead to play up the incident with the student.

"Why are you throwing away a masterpiece?" I held up the crumpled paper for the "artist" to see. "This looks like great sculpture to me." My jest gave way to a second look, and I suddenly did see linear movements that prompted me to place the crumpled paper carefully on a desk and to pull out my camera for a picture. (Photo 1.) When the student saw me seriously setting up equipment and heard the whirr of the camera, he came over with a suspicious look in his eyes.

"Hey, is this for real?"

"Sure! It's the greatest!" By this time the whole art class was watching. I glanced quickly at the teacher, and he waved me on. The class waited for some trick to appear. For a moment I wished I had a magic wand to meet their expectations, but then I decided that the invisible truth made visible was greater than the best magician's trick.

"I'm going to show you something that I think is amazing. This little piece of paper is playing a piece of music, and I can hear it. If you will let me show you, I think you can hear what I am hearing."

"He's putting us on," someone whispered.

I tried to show the boy with the crumpled "art" the basic idea of a Hogarthian line, a lyric line with two reversing curves.

Then I showed him how the biggest pattern in the paper sculpture followed a Hogarthian line, and I told him that for centuries sculptors had used a line like this down the center of their sculpture to bring life into their work, somewhat like music. On a piece of paper I drew some lines similar to the lyric lines of a girl's hair. (Photo 2.) Both hair and paper had the Hogarthian curve, but the inner curve of the paper sculpture held dozens of smaller lines with sharp points caused by the stiffer paper. Those sharp, hard-edged folds were somewhat like syncopation in the movement of lines. I tried giving a vocal impression of a

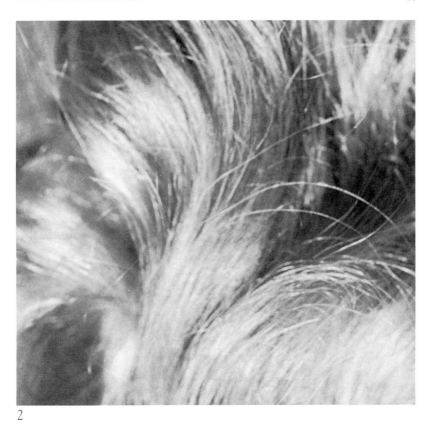

2

Latin American rhythm as I traced the syncopated track of the line along the crumpled edges. Hair and cloth do not have these syncopated characteristics because they are limp or lyric; thus they have a different visual rhythm. The boy seemed to catch on immediately as he saw in his paper sculpture the sound of rock music, and a humming lullaby in tresses of flowing hair.

His sculpture did have visual music. I think he heard it; he smiled with a distant look in his eyes. But we should remember, art is not an accident. We were exploring a perceptive aware-ness of art characteristics.

With this start on the search for visual music in common objects, many adventures are possible. Cabbage, for instance, has a different rhythm than hair or paper. (Photo 3.) The main linear pattern is still a Hogarthian curve, but the supporting lines have no sharp edges of paper and no smooth flow of hair strands. The cabbage exudes neither a lullaby nor a cha-cha. To me, cabbage lines slurp and burp their rhythm.

Turkeys, silver dollars, and crumpled paper all have rhythm to sensitive eyes. Vision of potential can place our youth on pedestals—but parents or grandparents of limited sensitivity might unknowingly bump some of our children into pitfalls.

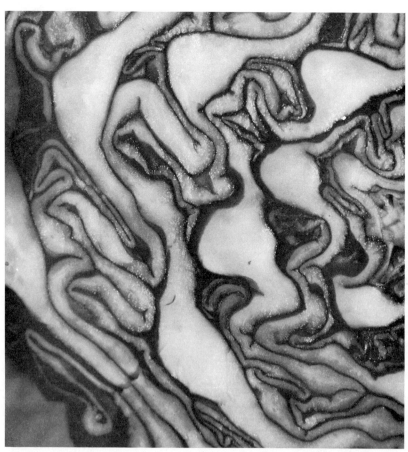

3

3

The Struggle for Spiritual Strengths

"For it must needs be, that there is opposition in all things. . . . All things must needs be a compound in one . . . happiness nor misery, neither sense nor insensibility." (2 Nephi 2:11.) Birth is countered by death; good is countered by evil; sensitivity is countered by barbarianism; aestheticism is countered by ugliness; the Lord's Spirit is countered by Lucifer's spirit. Strength, indeed survival, comes in the unity of positive spiritual things.

The spiritual thermometer that measures a life was warm despite the physical temperature of the bitterly cold night in Tibet. The approaching storm screamed down the pass toward two struggling figures in the snow. Wise to subzero travel, Sadhu Sundar Singh and his Tibetan companion knew they could not huddle for even a brief moment behind the icy fingers of rock that seemed to be clutching the white blanket of snow up to the earth's chin for some protection against the plunging temperature.

Suddenly the travelers stumbled over a body. A quick investigation revealed a few life signs remaining in the stiffening form. Sadhu, one of the first Christian converts in Tibet, quickly assessed the situation and, without hesitation, hoisted the stranger onto his back. The Tibetan companion cupped his hand near Sadhu's ear and cried his protest: "This is fate. It is destined that the fallen man should die here in the snow. It is destined that we should push forward!" Sadhu's hand shielding his face from the stinging cold did not hide his confident smile. This was no question to wrestle with. Firm with the confidence of a man who believed all things, who could endure all things, and who felt a deep Christian responsibility for his fellowman, his answer was clear and undebatable: he could not leave the stranger to freeze and die.

Leaning into the slicing wind with his human burden pushing him even deeper into the snow, Sadhu pressed forward. His companion refused to keep the slower pace and was soon lost to view in the thickening night.

Sadhu's burden grew heavier with each step. Not only did the increased effort strain his already aching muscles, but his heavier breathing sucked in the biting cold to the very pit of his lungs, sharpening the edge of pain. Despite the freezing air, perspiration began to run down his back. His body cried for relief, but Sadhu was determined. When he had long passed the second mile of endurance he still would not shed his burden to the frozen wasteland. The pain became numbness, and soon only his magnificent belief moved his legs. At the complete limit of all a man could endure he glimpsed a light in a crevice of the storm; it was the light of his destination. One final effort implored his fading consciousness to hold fast when he stumbled over a second body. The face that stared up in frozen death was that of his former companion.

The shock cleared Sadhu's aching mind. He who had sought to save his own life had lost it. Bracing himself against the blizzard, Sadhu again felt sweat on his back and shoulders under his fur coat, and suddenly he realized that his increased exertion and the warmth of the human burden he had risked his life to save had saved his own life.

Sadhu's spiritual convictions gave uncommon strength to his physical being. To those unable to accept the divine elements of a religious life, it may not be easy to understand the strengths that come from the gift of the Spirit, but it must at least be recognized that something happens in lives endowed with spirit that lifts them above natural physical limits. To tap that something, be it a religious or a psychological power, is surely a worthy pursuit, for it not only brings great strength in a crisis, but can permeate every facet of life and lead to the ultimate joy of human existence.

Indeed, the spirit that gives vitality and meaning to our lives also gives vitality and meaning to art. But what is this spirit?

Spirit seems to move independently of matter, while physical things move according to the principles of physics. A finer differentiation has been made: the Prophet Joseph Smith declared, "There is no such thing as immaterial matter. All spirit is matter, but it is more fine or pure, and can only be discerned by purer eyes; We cannot see it; but when our bodies are purified we shall see that it is all matter." (D&C 131:7-8.)

Art helps me to understand this concept, and this concept helps me to understand art. Art is not obvious physical element, such as paint or stone. Art is not what paint or stone is crafted to represent—trees, people, or abstractions. Art is something the eye must learn to see; what is eventually seen is the *spirit* of the work. Sadhu understood the Christian message, but as he became more sensitive to nonphysical elements and felt the spirit of the message, he was nurtured beyond warmth, beyond mortality; he was nurtured to see or feel eternal matter.

There are many evidences of spirit and many interpretations of those evidences. The purer our vision, the clearer our
interpretation. The religious skeptic who comes to appreciate
the spiritual in art may yet recognize that religion, like art,
cannot be judged solely on physical elements; in the final
analysis religion is a spiritual experience and can only be judged
by the spirit. If the skeptic hangs his case against religion on
people, on the physical elements of doctrine, without reaching
for spirit, he cannot understand religion any more than a
person who will not reach below the surface of the paint can
understand art.

If we want to understand a Frenchman in Paris we do not
demand that he speak English—we learn *his* language. If we
want to understand God, we need to learn a spiritual language
that comes with a purified body and an eye that can see a finer
matter. If we want to understand art, we need to learn the
language of the art spirit.

A search for sensitivity in art helps one to see more clearly.
But an artist with an understanding of aesthetic spirit still needs
the spiritual depth that Sadhu discovered. Nor can Sadhu,
even in the top of the Himalayas, afford to miss the aesthetic
sensitivities that help us understand the language of beauty and
the concomitant sensitivities for the eyes; one of my favorite
scriptures beautifully expresses this: "Consider the lilies of the
field, how they grow." (Matthew 6:28.)

The skeptical world hurls so many challenges at our beliefs
that it is possible to lose our grip on spiritual things or to accept
the ugly. Our mental and emotional equipment is bombarded
throughout our lives because we rationalize nonspiritual
positions. We need to draw ammunition for this bombardment
from all spiritual sources—the fine arts as well as religion.

The evil side of spirit penetrates the arts as well as many
religious organizations. Modern miracles of communication,
transportation, medicine, space science, and electronic commerce are all so impressively visible that a belief in an invisible
spirit, or God, may seem a bit unimportant. The buffeting of a

Tibetan storm that dominated the immediate environment of Sadhu Sundar Singh could not shake his spiritual convictions. But many of us have not yet achieved such spiritual fortresses against the storm.

A professor from Cornell University told of his distress at watching young students who had been well-protected from the winds of the outside world having their faith destroyed by some professors with a small breeze of a few simple ideas. The professor said that if those students had only gained more breadth in their learning while they were building their column of spiritual faith, they could have easily weathered the ideological storm and gained spiritual strength at the same time.

A visitor from a large cosmopolitan city said the same thing about some young people who had come there for work and who were unable to defend themselves adequately under a blizzard of moral pressures. Adamantly he declared that something must be done to prepare future youth to meet cold realities with greater strength. Isolation is not the answer.

To walk near the rubble of shattered spiritual lives is more distressing to me than to see broken or frozen physical bodies. And the face of America is becoming covered with such spiritual debris.

A leader of a citizen's group fighting pornography was asked to appear on a television panel with the operator of a theater that showed X-rated movies. The theater operator said his films met the legal test of having "redeeming artistic values." The citizen challenger asked him how he could make such a statement.

"They have plot," he replied with a shrug, indicating, "that's enough."

Because of such thin criteria to defend spirit-destroying films, we need community concern with more aesthetic judgments, not only to defend but to encourage things of higher spirit.

There are many different spiritual ladders we can climb. Each higher rung will bring new sensitivities into view. The day

I discovered color, not just *saw* color, I took a step up on a column of art spirit that offered me new color horizons. As I look up the ladder of art I can see still brighter lights far above me, reaching so high that I realize I will never stand side by side with Rembrandt, Francesca, or Zuniga. But that is no reason for me to stop climbing. The Christ, standing high above us on a column of divine spirit, expects us to keep climbing to perfection.

The column of divine spirit will always reach higher than that of any other form of spirit. On this column I have felt a clear answer to prayer. I have felt the Holy Spirit give me physical strength beyond my capacities. When we tap that spiritual power, we stand higher than the great art masters on their columns of aesthetic spirit. From my present position on this shaft of purer spirit I cannot see the top. Enoch is up there on a much higher level: "Enoch looked; and from Noah, he beheld all the families of the earth." (Moses 7:45.) Artists of keenest vision could not match that feat. Moses must be very high on this shaft; his capacity to be spiritually sensitive was awesome: "Moses cast his eyes and beheld the earth, yea, even all of it; and there was not a particle of it which he did not behold, discerning it by the spirit of God." (Moses 1:27.)

An artist's discerning mortal eye cannot approach a spiritual eye. There is a purer light in a spiritual eye (as explained in Luke 11:34). The scriptures tell us that to gain this spiritual light, we must have a mighty change in our hearts. A mighty change can not come about through apathy. Because spirit is a part of all things, we must include all aspects of life if we intend to search out and find enough spiritual strength to be mighty. To be mighty is not only to gain the great spiritual light the scriptures promise; it is to take up armor against the slings and arrows of daily life. Keeping the commandments of any spiritual law prepares the heart for a mighty change, but the scriptures also note that even the mighty can fall. The simple way for me to understand this is to think of what happens when a young man away from his family finds himself surrounded by companions whose character is good even if they do not have his same religious beliefs. Contrast this with the situation if he were surrounded instead by companions of negative character.

The defense that I suggest is that we learn to quicken our perception of spiritual elements in our environment, and that we live with that sensitivity, which includes having companions of like sensitivity. Then we will form a spiritual armor that improves our chances for survival. Any experience that dulls a child's sensitivity in any form should be a concern.

One who has built a column of wholesome art alongside his column of divine spirit has more armor against art that is spiritually destroying. To simply tell a youth to avoid art because some art is evil does not build armor and hopes for sanctuary. Safety comes when the child is spiritually mighty, surrounded with wholesome armor forged in several spiritual fields.

The Lord has asked us to make a serious study of scripture, but he has also urged us to undertake other study. (See D&C 88:118; 90:15; 93:53.) If our study of other subjects is integrated with the spirit of the central column as well as with our own natural spirits, the central column can be well protected.

The idea of getting spiritual support from various fields of study and experience has an important companion idea that started in the Garden of Eden. The first man and woman could do no evil, nor could they achieve anything good; there was no possibility for growth. Adam and Eve made a spiritual sacrifice that drove them from the garden and exposed them to evil. But where there could now be great evil, there was a companion possibility of great good.

From the beginning the family has been the cornerstone of society and the plan of eternity. Some of the greatest evils of the world are related to the family, just as some of the greatest goods are related to the family.

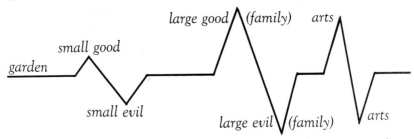

A look at the arts today seems to show almost as wide a swing as we find when we examine the family. Drama can rise with Shakespeare or it can slink to the low level of the so-called adult movie. The visual arts can rise with Michelangelo's *Moses* or skid down to pornography. Music can ascend with Handel's *Messiah* or thud with the vulgar lyrics of "sex rock."

The arts, as much as any activities outside religion, can lift a civilization or lead to its decline. The artworks of a falling empire become increasingly inferior with a loss of spirit. The arts of any culture or individual clearly reveal where that group or person stands on the scale of civilization; a group's arts also clearly reveal its spirituality.

We make a choice between good and evil with every influence we meet. If children learn through their experiences to make good choices, they will be more inclined to make good choices as adults. If children are given no education in the arts and faith, they may arrive at the age when they can enter "adult arts" and it will be too late to provide aesthetic or spiritual armor.

Parents who want their children to develop a taste for the spiritually beautiful cannot begin too early. I disagree with a book I read that said children cannot appreciate the beautiful. When my youngest daughter, Candy, was four years old, she accompanied me on a sabbatical leave. She was with me when I painted over seventy pictures, and we visited over a hundred art museums. One day we were driving over the crest of a hill when Candy cried, "Stop, stop, stop." I slammed on the brakes, thinking she was sick. As I turned to her she pointed out across the countryside and said softly, "Look how beautiful!" And it was.

She has continued to find beautiful things. We have had many discussions on what is good and what is poor in art. She loves a good art gallery, and she completely avoids degrading entertainment. She loves church meetings, the scriptures, and her church teachers. She carries a bright spirit into her religious study and into her contacts with friends and school subjects. Candy's central spiritual shaft of the Church is high, light, and well-fused into each column of her life's pyramid. I know art has helped. I know she can face heavy storms well-protected by her spiritual armor.

"He that ascended up on high, as also he descended below all things, in that he comprehended all things . . . the light of truth; Which truth shineth. This is the light of Christ . . . the light of the stars, and the power thereof . . . even the earth upon which you stand . . . the light which is in all things, which giveth life to all things, which is the law by which all things are governed, even the power of God who sitteth upon his throne. . . . And the spirit and the body are the soul of man." (D&C 88:6-15.)

Part II
Home Is More than a Hat Hanger

4
Key Words for Family Fixing

*Brambled paths need sharp tools. Let
us look at three key words that can help
prune brambles and at the same time
provide guidance in the search for
sensitivity and spirit.*

The conclusions of a lifetime form the philosophy and testimony that push up peaks of personal convictions. From my experience I assert that *spirit* is the most significant word in our language. Tied to that conviction is a belief in the importance of two other words, *sensitivity* and *identification*. Sensitivity grinds and polishes the lenses that enable us to see spirit. Identification sharpens our focus and relates our understandings.

There is another critical word in teaching: *growth*. *Growth* is a broad word that encompasses aesthetic, creative, emotional, perceptive, physical, social, mental, and spiritual aspects of life. Parents and grandparents who want to promote full growth, or who want to teach any lesson to another human being, must first establish concrete hooks or connections between the learner's experiences and the concepts to be learned. No matter how thorough learning may be, it will have no importance in a person's life until he has established identification.

For example, imagine you are a teenage boy. You come home from high school one afternoon and discover that your mother has bought a new telephone table because the old one was too small to accommodate an elbow while one was talking on the phone.

You shout, "Hey Mom, this new table is neat! Now we have room to write a phone message!" Seeing the phone reminds you that you have not talked to your girl friend, Audi, for two days. Dialing Audi's number with a pencil, you study the table, and then Audi's soft voice on the other end of the line suddenly blots out pencil, table, Mom, schoolwork, and house. Audi completely fills your world.

In this conversational world of floating clouds, a kind of crystal ball forms in the circular wood-grain pattern of the new table. Your eye absently sees the whole scene in the pattern, and somehow the pencil in your hand begins to trace round and round the lines of the wood grain.

Whack!

"What on earth are you doing to my new table?" The pink, cloudy castles of conversation pop with the slapped hand, and your eyes suddenly focus on the pencil-damaged table. Wetting your finger, you rub the mar, hoping that somehow you will make it disappear.

"I'm awful sorry, Mom; I just wasn't thinking. I'll be more careful with your table."

In a few moments Audi again fills your mind, and as you float back to your castles in the clouds, the power of a piece of design hypnotizes your eye, and the pencil returns to its former track.

Whack again!

"I can't imagine what is getting into you! You are deliberately disobeying me. Look at my new table!"

"I didn't mean to . . ."

"Didn't mean to! Just three minutes ago you said you were sorry and wouldn't do it again. Now it is worse than ever. Look!"

Keep this incident in mind for a few minutes, and let's pretend again. This time there is a little pioneer family that has traveled by covered wagon halfway across the United States to build a home in the West. The first priorities are to get a roof over their heads and crops in the ground. I can picture the family sitting on rocks or logs with dishes for their evening meal held in their laps. The mother turns to her husband and asks the same question she asked the previous week: "When will we be able to have a table? I want us to live like human beings again." I can imagine the pioneer woman's joy when her husband says, "We'll make a table tomorrow."

In the wilderness there is no store to provide tables; this is a family affair, and everyone helps with the project. The children watch as their father struggles to cut down a large tree. Each child helps remove branches and watches as the father cuts the trunk into planks. The children find and use abrasives to smooth the plank surfaces, and they hold the wood while their father makes joints. Mother meanwhile prepares varnish to seal the wood. Like a cherished gift, the finished table is joyfully carried into the log cabin by both children and parents, and that night a pleased mother serves dinner on a *table*. Mother is not the only family member who touches the new table top lovingly.

Imagine that somehow after dinner a telephone is suddenly available on the table, and the teenage pioneer boy decides to call his girlfriend, Audi. He might experience the same castle in the clouds, but it is unlikely that his reverie from the world will, or can, blot out the table. Something will hold back the hand with the pencil no matter how wonderfully the voice on the telephone line captures him. That something is identification.

The pioneer boy went through a "primary experience" with a table. Primary experiences reach out hooks and make identifications. The boy in the modern home experiences the table on a "secondary level"; he has not even gone with his mother to the store, and the detached level cannot reach through his girlfriend's voice to hook in.

Parents who hold family home evenings with their children could well remember the importance of primary experiences. Most families today may not build a table together, but there are many other activities that can create family identifications: the meaning of a Christlike life, the Church, democracy, school subjects, the arts, respect for other people, integrity, or the family itself—an endless range of topics.

A family identification experience for us started one day when I pulled a sorry-looking luggage trailer into our driveway in preparation for a trip to California, where I would attend graduate school. My family surveyed the sad sight. No one smiled. My bargain melted.

With a resolve to brighten the situation, I went to a paint store and purchased a heavy paint guaranteed to cover anything. Before the lid was even off the paint can the children excitedly gathered around to help paint. I could have said, "Children, your father is an art major. Sit right here, and you can watch an art major's fine paint job." They probably would have watched for as long as it took me to make two strokes. Instead I called for their mother, and she joined the project.

The children put on my oldest shirts for paint smocks; Jeanne tied bandanas around the girls' long hair, and we were ready. I showed the children how to spread newspaper on the garage floor, how to pull the excess paint off the brush. They responded with enthusiasm. Then I left them to the task. A little angel dressed in paint later came to beam that the trailer was finished. Jeanne and I went to admire the gleaming results.

The children's faces were as bright as the trailer.

The cleanup job was not as exciting as the painting had been, but when it was done I was impressed by the way the children sat around the trailer and admired the paint job. A radiant spirit surrounded the trailer. Most impressive of all to me was that as we drove off to California the children kept looking back at the trailer. It was no longer their daddy's trailer: it was *our* trailer. The *our* made a big difference. This identification experience helped unify our family.

One of the best family home evening identification experiences I know of was planned by the Christensen family. They chose a large tree as the site for a family home evening lesson. They rigged up a hammock for the mother, and put up a pulley or two to achieve lift-off. The father perched on one big branch facing the children, who were scattered throughout the branches on the other side. Then, manual in hand, the father gave the lesson.

Every time I think of this incident I delight in the imagination of this family and the many kinds of identification these children received. I suspect that as the children grow they will seldom walk into the backyard of their childhood home without a special look at that tree, and they will remember the time the family was together in the branches—an identification of a true togetherness experience.

Hearing about the California family made such an impact on me that I surveyed my own locality for a special family night. In the mountains east of our home is a craggy rock called Squaw Peak; overhearing the children talk about climbing it decided the site selection. (Photo 4.)

After a preliminary exploration for the best and safest route, our family safari started up the mountain on a Monday afternoon. We paused on the summit to watch the sun set across the valley far below, and we watched without speaking as a dark blanket was pulled across the valley bed. The lake formed a disk of gold in the blanket as it reflected the glowing burst of color in the sky.

As the doors between night and day came closer together, our voices could not remain still. We felt the need to point out to each other the changing scenes. The gold faded into the velvet black blanket, which soon became dotted with diamonds of light from the homes far below.

Our family night on top of Squaw Peak was one of our most memorable. The lesson was on building our lives upon a rock.

4

From our rocky perch the lights of the temple below were a steady visual beam that represented other kinds of rocks. Each person told of strengths he or she had found.

At an appointed hour we signaled with a flashlight to our neighborhood, and those who knew of our plans and were waiting for the signal flashed back their winking lights in the valley below. The responding light flashes—a link across the void—caused a leap within our beings that we have not forgotten. There were lessons of faith and of spirit in this silent communication.

Slipping into our sleeping bags, we realized the rocky summit was no cushion, but the exhilaration of our experience was

5

comfort enough. Often since that night I have seen the children look at the mountain in a new way: it is now *our* mountain. (Photo 5.)

Identification is a key word in a family tool chest.

The words used by the *Oxford English Dictionary* to define *spirit* and *sensitivity* are strikingly similar to the expressions used to describe art, religion, personality, adventure, and self-realization. If we take out of our memory banks the cards that are punched with our most exciting moments, the words on each card are the same.

The similarities between spiritual and temporal experiences can be used in teaching. These interrelationships provide an endless storehouse of identification links. The Master Teacher knew of this storehouse, and often used parables to provide identifications in the disciples' lives with the spiritual concepts he taught.

The definitions of spirit include *energy*. Spirit generates more spirit. A visit to the German Technical Museum in Munich convinces the viewer not to settle for a one-cylinder power source: on display are the numerous methods man has used to make energy. There are treadmills for human feet, water wheels, steam engines, modern turbines, atomic power. What a waste of human potential to put us back on the tread-mill and to ignore modern technology. Correspondingly, what a waste to accept a narrow view of spirit.

Some people are quite content with their lives as they feed spiritual needs from shallow sources. Anyone who has tapped the Holy Spirit is aware of such people's shortsighted percep-tions. For those who want to know, identification is a great tool in searching for a testimony of the gospel. An identification experience seldom comes in the form of a miracle; the scriptural advice is to "study it out in your mind." Such a study is primarily a search for identification links. These links are best made in family and home experiences.

There are some who do not understand the arts. Among those who are content to live their lives without aesthetic in-fluence are some who feel that since they have gained a testi-mony of the Holy Spirit, there is no need for anything else. Our mortal lives, however, were divinely designed to allow us a wide range of experiences. The greater our growth, the greater our capacity to identify with many areas of human and spiritual ex-perience. The larger our field of experience, the greater our capacity for growth. The family tool chest should not be limited just to basic tools.

Finally, each of us is so capable of learning errors that some safeguards should be included in our search. We can identify with faulty perceptions as well as with sin and crime. Even the best thinkers disagree on how we perceive. Learning to identify with good things is essential if we seek eternal progress. The greater the number of good things with which we can identify, the greater is our security. Discrimination is possible only if we are sensitive enough to discern spiritually.

If the family tool chest could have only one tool, I think it should be a sensitive identification with many forms of spirit.

5

Inside the Front Door

*We have explored a few paths to
sensitivity and spirit through the expressions of children and through the ways
we learn to express and anchor our own
experiences. These paths suggest the
value of a closer look at the family as a
source of "primary experiences" for
identification with things of spirit.*

The Japanese of former days understood the nurturing of
children. Important things were taught in the Japanese home:
worship of gods and ancestors, love of family, and enjoyment of
the beautiful.

One of my memorable experiences was to see a little
Japanese mother, immaculately clad in traditional dress, carry-
ing reverently a single flower. She moved across the room with
small, delicate steps to the *tokonoma*, a little alcove the Japanese

use as a beauty spot. With the poise of a polished dancer, and with infinite grace, she slowly lowered the flower into a small vase.

Her intensity captured her children's attention as they paused in their play and watched the simple ceremony. If the mother had stalked roughly across the room and shoved a fistful of flowers into the most convenient bowl, the children would have missed the sensitive lesson of mother's caring for something above food, clothing, and shelter. Her display of sensitive feelings to her children was a gentle teacher, but children quickly learn this kind of sensitivity when it comes early enough and frequently enough.

The Orientals have a long tradition of family caring and empathy development. It is no coincidence that most Oriental children have strong filial attachments. These family ties do not come by accident, nor are artistic sensitivity and appreciation due to chance. Unfortunately, since Japan became a leading industrial nation her families have taken on many occidental patterns and this empathy has lost some of its anchor.

Ancient China was the mother of Japanese sensitivities. Out of this past came an idea about the spirit of a home. Each room was expected to have a plant growing in it. A room was never considered empty of spirit if it contained a growing plant. Oriental children led artfully to this sensitivity could detect a vitality in the home that children reared with plastic flower decorations miss. Plastic flowers and other nonliving objects that don't require care may influence us into not caring about children's small needs.

Many apparently inconsequential items mold our sensitivities and influence our outlooks. Flowers may seem a small thing, but I found out while my children were still young that flowers were important to them. We had been camping out for several months while I was studying in European art galleries, and the burden on our one vehicle became large enough that we decided to buy a small trailer.

Exploring various models of trailers was an exciting

adventure for our children, although Jeanne and I were shopping only with thoughts of budget and weight. An eruption of childish exclamations indicated that our children had found their favorite. We hurried to see. Their choice was not affected by budget or weight, nor was their winner the trailer with the best bathroom facilities, the softest beds, the most space, the most gadgets, or the most chrome. Their choice was the trailer with flowers on the table! Our children were sitting around the table when we found them, and their smiles told us that it seemed like home. Our trip had provided us with many adventures, but their faces ringing the table told me more than their tongues that they had found ties with home, something that was more important to me than any adventure.

I looked at the flowers and felt uncomfortable. They were

6

plastic and without life. (Photo 6.) They would never grow better; only the dust on them would change. But then I realized that if imitations could move children, and those children in turn could move their father, what potentials we could uncover if we helped our children appreciate more than a plastic petal, more than a soft petal, but growth itself.

Caring for small things that live is an important family lesson that can transfer into caring for people. Caring for unseen growth may transfer into caring for unseen divine things.

Our family will not forget a little Dutch boy who came to our rescue on a stormy night when our car was stalled on a lost lane. A light down the lane led me to his door. I was chilled and drenched from the rain, and I welcomed the invitation inside to an immaculate home.

Anxious to share my problem, the Dutch family gathered around a table holding a beautiful floral arrangement. As they talked with each other in a way that showed deep family roots, the boy reached out and with great feeling touched a petal of the flower arrangement.

Later I clung to the boy as we sliced through the rain at midnight on his motorbike in search of a gas station. The gas we finally found did not start the car; there was nothing else we could do. We waved goodbye to him, and as he disappeared in the storm our hopes slid to zero.

The rain continued to drum on the metal roof of the car, and I found my fingers tapping in response on the dashboard as I tried to devise some plan. No plan came—only rain to increase our feelings of isolation. Our schedule was critical, and my agitation grew with the puddles around the car. Then far up the lane in the rain we noticed two red lights. As the lights grew bigger we could see that they were followed by a truck, which was backing toward our car. Within a few minutes a chain was hooked to the bumper. Somehow the Dutch boy with a second-mile effort had found a friend with a truck. For at least forty-five minutes we were pulled blindly through the storm.

At last we rolled to a stop in front of a large garage. No lights were burning, but several waving arms at the door told us we were expected. The driver of the truck would accept nothing for his services; his manner and words communicated his enjoyment in helping strangers in distress. Then I noticed on his dashboard a vase of living flowers.

Lights blazed on as the garage door opened and our car was pushed inside. The mechanic and his family had come to open the garage at one o'clock in the morning; they also had warm refreshments ready for us. Not one of them seemed irritated by the inconvenience.

Soon the broken engine part was replaced and the motor was running smoothly. Smiles were everywhere. To make a financial settlement I went to the office, where I found a vase of flowers brightening the desk.

As we drove off into the cold storm with a chorus of good-byes, the wind and the rain meant nothing; we had conquered the storm because we had felt the warmth of people who cared. We asked ourselves how so many people could show such genuine interest in strangers in the middle of a cold rainy night. Somewhere the Dutch have learned sensitive lessons of caring. When I look at the flowers of Holland I can see the source of sensitivity.

Flowers in any home provide an atmosphere of sensitivity and beauty, but it is the *caring* for the flowers that makes the atmosphere truly beautiful.

Many other objects in a home influence the home's spirit. In our home I have a "spirit stick" hanging on the hall wall. A jungle guide once told me that spirit sticks are driven into the ground to quicken the earth spirits during the planting season in New Guinea. To the native their power is awesome. I don't personally recognize that power, but I do find a powerful spirit of artistic expression in the stick's design that complements such power. My admiration for the stick's aesthetic qualities prompts me to display it on the wall. My children walk by it with hardly a flicker of interest; as far as they are concerned, it means nothing, because they have no identification hooks with the stick. For them it only adds to the room's visual clutter.

Cast a critical eye over the things in your living room. How many of them have links with an experience of your children or grandchildren that will make these objects interesting? If you see none, your living room needs some changes. When a child paints a picture and you hang it on the wall, it makes the room important to the child.

Living rooms are also for adults, and your interests should have a place in the room. But do your interests link with those of other family members? We miss valuable teaching moments with our families if we fail to explain our treasures in a way that will ignite our family members' interests. Mutual sharing creates family unity.

Before we make identification hooks to our memorabilia, however, we need to be sure the memorabilia are worthy. If they are not worthy of a sensitive taste, they are visual litter, despite the dressing we give them. The only thing we accomplish is that we foist onto the child an appreciation of inferior things.

The search for sensitivity and spirit in a home is something of a brambles-and-buttercup experience. Things like flowers affect the sensitivity and spirit of our homes, whether home is a one-room apartment or a mansion on an estate. Other things can hurt the sensitivity or spirit. Any person—father, mother, child, or single adult—who desires a better living environment and who has had limited experience in aesthetics may face a flowers-or-brambles situation in the home, somewhat like the new gardener who hopes he is pulling weeds instead of plants from his first garden.

The first step in distinguishing between brambles and buttercups in the home is to recognize the spiritual implications of everything in the home and to recognize the intangible spirit of the family itself. The second step must be to help family members identify with these things. This is a critical step, which includes the need to identify with the best elements and to reject the inferior ones. Parents who care about the home environment but who are unaware that they are visually insensitive may teach their children to care for the mediocre or the aesthetically offensive.

Identifications often come without our doing anything. The enjoyment of the mediocre or the artistically inferior is a dubious step up for those who are content to live with unswept trash and without visual enjoyment.

As we grow older and our own growth brings our experience into focus, we often look back and lament things we wish we had done for our children. I keep wishing that I had used nature's small masterpieces to add interest in the home, that I had given my children more modern dance experiences with a perceptive Virginia Tanner, had made a *tokonoma* in our home, had held better family home evenings with the children sooner, had given them more exciting experiences with textures and other sensory stimuli. I hope that something in these pages may help young parents become more aware of the signposts I did not see.

The home is a complicated arena. Its spirit is a product of design and function, of delicate personality mixtures, of religious ethics, of sociological impacts of community and friends, of traditions, of government regulations, and of economic pressures. The spirit in a home is, of course, a product of the love that tied the first knot in creating that home. Many have said that the home is the most important factor in shaping an individual, a community, or a nation.

How important is the spirit of the home? Studies of infants have led researchers to conclude that even small stimuli in the home contribute to the child's growth. How we talk to a child, the amount of time we spend with him, the visual experiences we bring into his surroundings, and even the way we present a learning experience to him—all these mold his life.

C. M. Corter of the University of North Carolina studied the closeness ten-month-old infants had developed with their mothers. Each baby was left with a toy in a room opening onto two other rooms. In one of these rooms was the infant's mother; in the other was a stranger. Only one baby crawled into the stranger's room and touched her. Every other baby revealed links he had established with his mother by smiling, crawling to her, and touching her.

Other studies substantiate the finding that environment is critical in providing the visual and intellectual stimulation that contributes to a child's growth, self-image, and security. It is vital that parents provide a healthy home environment.

A starting point in creating such a home environment is to write down family goals. These goals affect household design. What are the major activities of the family? Sleeping, eating, and bathing obviously head the list. Other important activities are study, hobbies, family nights, family projects, religious activities, art appreciation, activities to promote health, and recreation.

The design of a home should be flexible enough to change from a nursery to a place where teenagers could practice dance or debate to a place that can meet the special needs of senior citizens. Married children may have their own homes, but grandchildren can learn and appreciate a great deal about their family by examining grandma's and grandpa's storehouse of treasures. One home I know of—nestled in a canyon—was designed with grandchildren in mind; it features hobby areas, a photography darkroom, and even a stage for children's plays. (Photo 7.)

Design that meets family needs can't help but contribute to a higher level of family spirit. Each family is unique in some way, and the home should express this uniqueness. The first principle of art is unity, and this kind of harmony in a home is a spirit builder.

Whether a person is an apartment dweller or a house builder, what goes into his home affects his children. Sensitivity in the home can start with the smallest trinket brought back from a trip, items displayed on shelves, pictures hung on the walls.

7

In choosing between beauty and visual litter, it may seem strange that a rusty blade of an old tool found in grandfather's plowed field can be more beautiful than most of the souvenir objects that litter tourist traps. A blade with a beautiful shape, fine proportion, and a speckling of rust may be pure pleasure to a sensitive eye. A souvenir from a tourist stand may evoke a memory of some favorite place, but if it is an object of poor craftsmanship, it is visual litter.

Children should not be exposed to inferior design. An even greater threat occurs when an inferior object is a reminder of a pleasant family experience; creating identification with objects of poor design robs the family of aesthetic growth.

At a popular American tourist center I watched many people purchase small covered-wagon lamps with landscape scenes painted on the canvas wagon covers. These lamps are a design mistake. Covered wagons were not intended to be picture frames, and a sensitive painter would not want the competition of a covered-wagon lamp for a frame.

Forcing together two items of different functions usually sounds the visual-litter alarm. Many items in homes are visually disturbing. A planter box designed to resemble a little automobile is not good design. (Photo 8.) An automobile is not intended to function as a container for growing plants; a container to grow plants is not intended to have headlights and roll around on wheels.

Once I saw a cactus growing in a little replica of grandma's rocking chair. Anyone who would sit in a chair that had cactus growing in the seat should surely get my point.

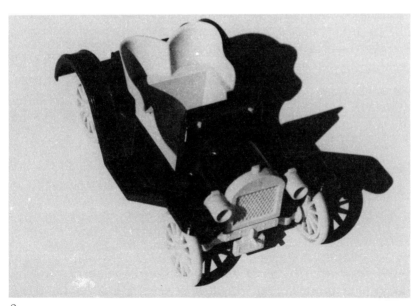

8

Let me sharpen the point. A cactus has a spirit of its own that bristles sharply, and to move among cactus plants requires that we keep a wary eye on where we back our sitting mechanism. A grandmother's chair is an open invitation to sit down and relax with a bit of rhythmical rocking. Those two spirits are decidedly opposite, and our bodies know it almost instinctively. To force these two spirits into a single object leads to a design collision. Although the rocking chair planter I saw was only ten inches high and no one can physically sit in it, the eye can, and the spirit can. If children are exposed to this design bramble, they will begin to identify with insensitive things.

Architect Louis Sullivan made a statement about design that has become very well known: "Form follows function." A whole design movement evolved from this statement; adherents called themselves "functionalists."

Let's look at this philosophy in a historical context. Along the Nile River before the pyramids were built, people made their homes from the mud and reeds they found along the river banks. Bundles of reeds were tied together into columns and then plaited into strands between the columns to make walls. The Egyptians then covered the structure with mud and dried it under the desert sun. This simple shelter met the functions of keeping the sun and heat away, of preventing sand from blowing into their belongings, of giving privacy from their neighbors, and of serving the other requirements of a dwelling place. A home like this was truly functional both in the purposes it served and in the natural use of materials.

When the Egyptians learned how to build with stone, it seemed natural for them to carve round corners on stone buildings; those round corners, laboriously chiseled from stone,

represented the tied reeds that had formed the corners of the baked mud houses. The round stone corner did not have the function of making the wall stronger; it was now simply a decoration. If the corner had been made to look as much like reeds as possible, it would have been a functional lie, because reeds could not support stone. We often make this kind of a design mistake. Realism in decoration has tremendous risks.

The part above the columns on a Greek temple is called the *entablature*—the cornice, frieze, and lintel. When skyscrapers were built it seemed natural to have the entablature on the top floor of the building. Modern architects thought this had also lost its function because it was so high above most of the windows that it gave no shelter from the sun or rain. Making it big enough to remain in scale would make it a threat to the people on the sidewalk below. People were startled when the modern architect removed this decoration. The architects believed it was no longer functional or decoratively desirable. The average person, however, thought that the shaved tops of the buildings looked naked and that the decoration was needed. Modern designers have in many ways cleared off excessive decoration, and today most people give no attention to a modern building without an entablature projecting from the top story. In fact, when an entablature is used, it tends to impart an old-fashioned flavor.

It was in the controversy over what was decorative and what was functional that Louis Sullivan made his statement on function. He was saying that the shape of an object must have a direct relationship to what the object does; the form must be consistent with the purpose. This means that a ship has a knife-edge bow to cut through water, not for decoration, and that a chair must be designed with the comfort of those sitting in it as a first consideration. I remember seeing a chair that was beautifully carved, but unfortunately, the carver's enthusiasm did not stop when he reached the seat. What was delightful to look at was not so delightful to sit on. In Sullivan's terms it was a poor example of design because the major functional requirement of a chair had been violated.

Fine artists strive to have each part of a design coordinate with all the other parts of the design; everything relates to a total sum. Having a tiny pair of ski boots for salt shakers or a miniature automobile as a planter is like wearing a tuxedo with football shoes.

A salt/pepper/sugar set at a local store caught my eye. The side of the container made this bold declaration: "At last, a centerpiece that is truly decorative and functional." Opening the box we found a gem of an example. (Photo 9.) How could the ad writer have ever considered this set functional? A pineapple has no function as a salt container, and a grapefruit surely has no relationship to pepper. One who wants to sweeten his cereal may never know that the sugar is hidden underneath the fruit unless he picks up the banana by mistake hoping that it is garlic, when it is really the sugar-bowl handle. (Photos 10, 11.)

The container copy continues: "The realistic color . . . " Those who have examined this salt-and-pepper innovation have agreed that the color looks realistically like plastic. "The

9

10

11

realistic color and artistic arrangement . . . " One of the fundamental rules of good decoration is that the base must be substantial enough to hold the decoration. This decoration completely overwhelms the structure that supports it.

By any aesthetic criteria I have studied, the statement on
the carton is a misrepresentation. In no way may the salt and
pepper set be considered an artistic creation; this set and all its
relatives are visual litter. Any parent who purchases a set like
this and exposes his family to the object *as an artwork* does
damage to the family's aesthetic growth.

But these criticisms must be kept in perspective: many
things can be fun and do not need to be artistic. We can make
visual puns of many items for their humorous value, but children must not be taught that visual puns are art.

Every family has some objects on display. Some of those
objects are seldom used, but are for eye pleasure alone: a vase of
flowers, a seashell, a glass bowl. Other objects are for utility:
radios, lamps, books, firewood holders. Though they are
objects of utility, they should meet their function while also
being pleasing to the eye.

A basic rule of thumb of decorating is that decoration
should enhance an object, not command it. All other elements
should support whatever the designer selects to be the star of
the show. When someone says that a bit player "stole the
show" they mean that the play was not well presented. A bit
player is intended to enhance the play, not to be the star. If he
is worthy to be the star, the play must be redesigned or roles ex-
changed. When a supporting cast member takes undue stage
presence, the leading actors lose their importance and the play
becomes muddled. If an object in the home is to enhance a
room, it cannot command the environment or it starts to
muddle the room. Visual litter is the result. No matter how
beautiful the color or shape of an object, the house is hurt if the
object commands the scene when it is not meant to be the "star
of the show."

If a house has too many distinctive parts, the eye becomes

unsure about where to look. This problem is called "visual disturbance." There needs to be some kind of a family resemblance among all of the parts of a house. (A family can have various kinds of disturbance too. If everyone is talking at once, the result is discord. Some stronger personality, such as a father or mother, needs to lead and to be a major influence if other members are to blend together.)

Within any room there should be some areas of greater attention and some areas of lesser importance. That difference in importance should not be too big; such a situation would resemble a four-star general leading only privates.

How objects are placed in a room is an important design consideration. If they look as though they were "placed there" rather than "left there," an achievement in sensitivity and design has been reached. But there is also a point when a too-rigid placing has problems. If nothing can be moved in a room, the home has lost its livability. If the room looks so sterile that no spirit lives within—let alone a family—the design has lost the key psychological ingredient: it does not have a personality, a spiritual essence.

The Impressionist painters wanted to create a "posed—not posed" quality in their pictures for similar reasons. Their casually posed pictures of people being natural were actually very studied and carefully placed.

Look at the various parts of a room critically with all these design elements in mind. Consider a room with a ceiling of exposed beams. In colonial times a builder would hand-tool the beams. The tools for the hewing task created a textural surface of great beauty. But labor costs today make the creation of hand-hewn beams too expensive. So to achieve an "authentic" effect, a modern builder desiring a colonial theme for a tract of homes in California had his workmen saw lumber clean with modern machinery and then hack a few pieces off the beam at intervals to suggest a hand-hewn quality. Our colonial ancestors made a functional beam with textural warmth; the modern builder's effect was really only a butchered beam.

Walls face our eyes so directly that they are major visual concerns. A family fond of nature may want a picture window, but if the opening exposes a view of the neighbor's garbage cans or a dirty alley, the owner might resentfully brick up the window. The living room now probably has the friendliness of a bastille; the wall is crying for decorative relief. Decorative enrichment to relieve the severe surfaces can raise a family's spirits considerably.

The design an artist uses in his artwork is the same kind of design a homemaker uses to make the home more beautiful and, even more important, to make a spiritual atmosphere that can influence children. Anything that influences children in right directions is gospel-oriented; this is another evidence to me that art is linked with the divine.

6

In Front of the Outside Door

*The search for sensitivity and spirit
needs no exotic land for exploration.
Every path from the family's front door
leads to opportunities for sensitive
discoveries.*

The purchase of a home usually becomes the single biggest visual investment of a young family's life. If the design of the house is a passing fad and public taste moves to other design interests, a homeowner required to move to a new locality may suddenly find that he is forced to sell his home at such a low price it will be impossible to finance a house of the same size and comfort in the new neighborhood. Design ignorance, then, can cost money as well as create visual litter.

Obviously, the design quality of a family's major purchases should be an important financial consideration. A trip through the residential area of most cities in America will reveal a large number of inferior designs in home construction. (Photo 12.)

12

Home design should have a focal point that leads the eye and provides a lively welcome to the entry. Where is the focal point on this house? The greatest design activity is on the garage doors. The strong diagonal crossing lines command entrance attention. In fact, they shout so loudly that it is difficult to look anywhere else.

Some shutters have been added to the garage doors to increase the design interest. Shutters were originally designed to fold over windows to keep out light or storms as well as to give a decorative enrichment. These shutters have obviously lost their historical function. Even if they were not nailed solidly to the garage, they would be too large for the size of the window. The shutters on the front wall of the house have a reverse mismatch: they are much too small to cover the windows.

The "cute" decoration on the roof is also prominent enough to join a circus. Its function is not clear and the question is often asked, "What is it?" Elements like these are too superficial to carry the spirit of a family home.

Look again at the photograph and imagine what or who should live in this house: the Gingerbread Man, Hansel and Gretel, Emily Post, or a Supreme Court justice? The outside of the house broadcasts a definite character — is it what the owner intended?

Textures are meant to provide interest, but there is an argument here as to which one is the winner. Count how many different kinds of textures are on the house without any one being the star of the show.

Louis Sullivan's famous student, Frank Lloyd Wright, used the term "organic design" to indicate that all elements of a piece of architecture, or of any artwork, should blend into one unit, and that all parts function together as a whole.

Wright disliked the term "applied art." He was opposed to the idea of making any object and then separately deciding what kind of decoration should be applied to the object to give it an enriched appearance. He firmly believed that if an object needed decoration it should be a part of the object's total design, and it should be integrated to meet the function of the object both physically and psychologically.

The house in the photograph gives the impression that the builder thought, "What else can I put on this house to make it look more impressive, more expensive or more fashionable?" These "mores" are all foreign to an organic design that would be built around the needs and aesthetic atmosphere of a family.

One of the sad facts about visual litter is our willingness to live with it even when it is recognized as visual litter. In our neighborhood we decided to erect a telephone pole to carry a street light. No one wanted to volunteer a spot for the pole, though. As each person repeated his reluctance to have the eyesore on his front lawn, one neighbor spoke up and said, "It won't make much difference; we'll soon get used to it." How true. It's a bit frightening to realize how quickly we accept the ugly.

The telephone pole discussion tuned up my awareness of poles. The next time I drove across the state I was looking for telephone poles, and I saw visual litter in a new way. I became sharply aware of how ugly is the design of many of our cities. I should like to make people upset with their ugly surroundings, for we shall never start to do something about them until we are aware and we are upset.

President Spencer W. Kimball has urged Church members for a long time to make their homes and yards more beautiful. The United States bicentennial year was filled with programs to meet similar objectives. Many participated in these programs who had already achieved both the sensitivity and the pride to free their living areas from visual litter and to create places of beauty.

But I cannot forget the association I had with a civic planner who hired me to do some graphics in community and home improvement. As we prepared a filmstrip pointing out the ugly elements that contributed to visual litter in our community, we found so many really bad examples to photograph that we were quite distressed.

One afternoon we sat in Dale's car and looked at a run-down, dilapidated house with a screen door hanging on only one screw. The family coming and going through the front yard did not seem to realize the ugliness that they had wrapped around themselves and forced upon their neighbors.

A set of rusty bed springs leaned against one outside wall; an old overstuffed sofa with most of its cotton batting falling out occupied the space along a front wall. A garbage can punctuated what was once a front lawn. Parts of automobiles were strewn here and there. Trash occupied the places between the bedsprings and the sofa. Children and parents leaving and entering the house did not even seem to see the trash.

Dale and I looked at each other dismally. We could not help but observe that at this low point of garbage-dump living, the home did not seem to have many bright spots. There were no smiling faces as the family members crossed the threshold. I worry about children who grow up in so much litter that living with trash becomes a natural part of their lives.

If we move up the litter-ladder there are home owners who *do* care about the appearance of their homes. The children come to know that their parents want to make the home attractive. Parents' attitudes rub off on most youth, even though the rubbing may not become evident until they own homes of their own.

The tragedy, however, is when parents care, but do not know how to make the area attractive. They may avoid trash, but there is a wide area of insensitive living that encourages a kind of aesthetic trash, and children learn to enjoy the mediocre or the aesthetically offensive. There is, of course, virtue in cleanliness, and order is design in itself.

Climbing higher on the ladder is the home owner who is aesthetically sensitive, who has a keen sense of caring for beautiful things and shares this with his children. The beautiful gardens and homes of the traditional Oriental cultures take aesthetic root in children's lives. A Chinese mother would, for example, make special efforts to lead her children into experiences of feeling jade. These lessons teach children not only to understand differences, but to appreciate quality and to enjoy such aesthetic qualities as tactile beauty. Stones to touch, stones to see, stones for strength in sculpture or architecture, stones to reach spirits: stones have many roles in our environment.

In addition to helping children by providing a sensitive environment, parents need to help in other ways. Too few parents nourish the young artists inside their children so that those children might be more aware of the excitement of texture. A woman who enjoys a soft fur collar or a man who wants some rugged stone near the entrance to his house have tasted this enjoyment. Do we lead children to sense these qualities?

Without artistic stimulation, children will likely grow up and put stones by their front doors just because their parents did. In too many cases they will do it with no sensitivity at all. Who will ask, "Why stone or why not stone?" "How big a

13

stone?" "How does the texture of the stone go with the other textures of the house?" "Where is stone best placed—near the house or in a garden?"

Ideas from the childhood home become part of the small artist inside each person, but without a sensitive development of taste, the adult makes strange combinations around the home, and at times the end product is nothing more than a blot on the environment.

For instance, there is a natural beauty in rocks. The Japanese were among the first to appreciate the aesthetic possibilities of arranging rocks; one of the most sensitive and artistic of these rock designs is the Roan-ji Gardens near Kyoto, where fifteen rocks rise in a symbolic sea of sand. (Photo 13.) I once led a tour group there, and after the necessary walk to the garden from the bus we paused at the border of this simple rock garden to catch our breath from the hot weather climb. Before I could say anything, one of the tour members gasped, "How much farther?"

"We are here. This is probably the world's best-known rock garden."

"That! You mean we came all this way just to see *that?*"

Several people in the group who had already been capti-vated by the poetry of the silent stones turned with quick frowns. On the risers to one side a Zen Buddhist sat in meditation, focusing his sight on the rocks almost as though they were seer stones. I suspect the Buddhist had been absorbed in his aesthetic study for a longer time than any of us were capable of sustaining. He was seeing through an educated spiritual awareness. Any visitor who felt that the garden lacked something was seeing through uneducated eyes.

Home builders who reject the litter of dirt and trash and enjoy well-trimmed lawns and flowered borders may still live in a visual litter of rocks. Gardens with stones are fashionable, and many of us have sweated and tugged to move our weighty decorations. Our intent is to create pleasure for the eye rather than an obstacle for the foot. But the eye can stumble in litter just as much as the foot can. Some rocks are more beautiful than others, but even the most beautiful rocks can be disturb-ing. This kind of disturbance would be like an exhibition of fine paintings haphazardly displayed, hung in sequence just as they came out of the crates and on whatever nails happened to be available. Anyone who can picture such confusion in an art gallery should immediately recognize that even magnificent rocks must be placed with good design relationships if we wish to create a thing of beauty. The sensitivity we use in arranging the stone by shape, size, color, texture, direction of the stone's thrust, amount of detail, and placement is what achieves the aesthetic beauty we should desire.

A simple approach to a rock garden is to select one rock as the star of the show and then some well-proportioned supporting cast members. Within the supporting cast there should also be a leader, but not one powerful enough to be in competition with the star. Even the rock with the least im-portance in a garden should have some point of emphasis within its own shape, such as a distinctive bump or dip. Good design considers every part. The prima donna of a ballet may be well placed and beautifully poised, but if all the others in the company are doing their own thing the stage will be visually distressing. Homes with distressing design quietly or emphatically disturb the occupants' spirits.

Spiritual design also considers every part of the whole. A family in Palo Alto, California, has mastered spiritual family design. In the evening the daughter goes to the piano to play a Church hymn when the hour approaches ten o'clock. As the family hears the music they find a breaking point in their study or personal activities and assemble around the piano to sing together. After singing a few hymns they then kneel together for family prayer. The father is a very sensitive man, and he often gives a sage thought before the prayer is offered. As they rise from their knees to retire for the night or to resume their various activities, another spiritual experience has been added to the home's bulging store.

On one occasion this family's oldest boy left a few days early from a family gathering at his grandparents' home to return to Palo Alto and pack for his first year at college. When the family returned home they found he had made a gift for each one of them. These gifts were not commercial items—in the pressure of packing he could have jumped in the car for a quick shopping trip, but he chose instead to create his gifts. He had hand-tooled belts for his brother and father, a plant hanger for his mother, and a purse for his sister. When the family returned, the boy's spirit was still there in gifts that were made as much with affection as with leather. In caring for each other, the family has been nurtured in caring for eternal things. The parents have truly given their children the "gift of the Spirit."

Part III

"If Men Were Fish the Last Thing They'd Discover Would Be Water"

7

The Ooohs and Ouches of
Community Sensitivity

A favorite teacher, I. James Quillen,
often told us, "If men were fish, the last
thing they'd discover would be water."
He wanted to stress that our culture
and environment, so close to us that we
hardly see them, powerfully influence
every part of our lives. The environment
around the home is a natural widening
of the search for spirit. The thorns are as
abundant in the community as they are
in the family residence.

One of the great privileges of my life was to hear architect
Richard Neutra lecture in Los Angeles. He was so impressive
that many of the audience members gathered around the

podium following his presentation to hear anything else he might say.

One person asked Neutra why architecture magazines had pictures of houses that looked as though no one lived in them. With a touch of a smile the architect replied, "Would you want a picture printed of your front room with shoes in the center, underwear strewn across the floor, and the dirty dishes from last night's refreshments on the table?"

His answer made sense, but the questioner pushed deeper: "Well, no, but the houses seem to be more a display of architecture than places for children to live."

No smile warmed Neutra's face this time. Almost as though someone had pulled the switch for a volcano to erupt, the great man started to tremble as he formed his words; they came bursting forth with great power: "What do you mean? Houses are *for* children!"

The room seemed to vibrate with his fervor. No one in the hall doubted that a sensitive nerve had been pricked; a deep suspense circled the group. As we waited we could sense Neutra mentally reviewing a mass of data for a topic that must have been close to his heart. Then he declared he would make an architectural defense of his answer by showing what architecture had done for children.

Neutra went to his slide box, did some quick sorting, and began projecting pictures of school buildings he had designed at least twenty years earlier. We were amazed: these schools looked as modern as any built today. Neutra felt that children should not be herded down a packed hall, crammed into drab rooms for verbal stuffing, and then pushed back into the halls for a noisy flight from school to do the things children would rather do. He believed that children were already part of the community, and that the school should spill into the neighborhood. He designed a classroom door that opened directly to the outdoors instead of into a congested hall. He also made the classroom so visually attractive that children would want to spill right back into the learning situation. A slanted ceiling would provide more light for the student stations farthest from the windows.

As Neutra presented numerous features designed with children in mind we were well convinced that he loved little folk and was concerned for their total well-being, which included all aspects of life—work, play, sharing, and a sensitive outlook.

When he switched off the projector, Neutra sat down, leaned back, and said he wanted to give us one of the most important lessons we would learn as artists, architects, teachers, and parents. He illustrated the lesson with an incident from his life.

As a child Richard Neutra had lived in Vienna. The living room in his parents' home was lighted at night by a coal-oil lamp placed on the central table. Near the wall was a couch with an unusual, poorly designed shape, and when the lighted lamp was on the table the couch cast an undulating, evil-looking shadow on the wall.

The intensity of Neutra's recollection drew our emotions closer to him. The picture he formed in our minds transported us from the podium spotlight to the flickering fear of lamp and shadow in a boy's midnight dreams. Neutra revealed that all through his childhood—and adult life as well—he had been startled out of sleep by frightening black shadows fluttering through his dreams. His home had become a cavern of fear.

Neutra looked straight at us and repeated that whether we were parents, artists, teachers, or architects, we had a responsibility to design our environment to give children pleasant dreams, to have children live and learn in the midst of beautiful design instead of visual litter. Neutra was the first person I heard use the expression "visual litter."

Leaving the lecture hall we returned to our hotel along the same street we had crossed on our way to the lecture, but Neutra's spirit now walked with us and the street seemed different. The buildings, the signs, the sidewalks, the street's whole nature had changed through our new awareness. I asked myself as I looked around, "What do I see that would give children beautiful dreams?" All I could see were neon nightmares; harsh, flashing lights surrounded with the gaudy glory of advertising signs competing for our attention. There was no lullaby for children on this street.

The lights edged buildings of undistinguished design to materialize into shadows that lurked in doorways and crept across small alleyways for new hiding places. As we turned the corner a black shadow, a horror-movie billboard, jumped out at us.

It was clear that the major impression of the clutter on this street was not to "please the eye and to gladden the heart . . . and to enliven the soul." (D&C 59:18-19.) Indeed, much on this street jabbed at the eye. Indifference to beauty spoke of hard hearts.

A motorbike without a muffler snarled down the street snagging every ear and turning every head to the audio litter. In a moment the rider was gone. The visual litter did not go away.

Leaving town the next day we drove along other streets that were even less attractive. Forced to stop in a traffic jam caused by poorly designed road systems, I studied a continuous row of apartment buildings with jumbled fronts and balconies strewn with brooms, boxes, and clotheslines in every direction. What dream materials were the children absorbing as they played among this visual debris? The insides of the apartments were not visible, but the overflow of materials onto the stairwells and balconies suggested ugliness within. Was I seeing one of Neutra's statements unfolding? Were the children being dulled in their homes? Would they then become adults dulled in their cities? Ghetto living produces too many ghetto minds and ghetto hearts.

Farther from the city center we drove past an expensive house guarded by a gate that was a visual horror. Both the style of the gate and the design of the wall belonged to the same "expensive club," but they were not good friends. The rich do not have a monopoly on good taste; visual litter is not a monopoly of the poor.

The eye-stinging cover of smog smothering Los Angeles squeezed out one blessing: agitated public awareness of pollution in many forms. Pollution became a dirty word. Smog in the late sixties had even seeped from the industrial centers of Europe into the green valleys of clean, hydro-powered Switzerland; the rich green was now veiled a gray-green. The innocent were being swept under the dirty blanket.

The time had arrived for citizens in concert to join the pollution pioneers and voice a world's concern over all kinds of environmental irritants. (Photo 14.) Community eyes awakened to visual irritants, and legislation was passed to remove billboards from along highways. Legislation also began to take down the visual clutter of main streets' bulky signs over sidewalks.

Architects began to make big city streets less like canyon walls. In spite of the high cost of property, space was reserved to give our spirits room to move; gardens and fountains can

14

15

16

now be found in front of tall buildings where there used to be only the visual monotony of concrete. The jumble of power and telephone poles has been placed underground. Much progress has been made in a quarter of a century. (Photo 15.)

But the battle against visual litter and pollutants has only begun. The bastille is still before us. During my last visit to New York City I had a grimy feeling. The subways were a mass of graffiti. Garbage and litter blew about the platforms with the winds of the arriving trains; winds from the streets above gathered more trash into clusters. Most distressing was the fact that no one seemed to care. (Photo 16.)

After a ghetto riot in Washington, D.C., we drove out to see the fire-gutted buildings. The neighborhood was tremendously depressing. Not a single touch of beauty was in evidence; there was only litter and futility. I kept asking myself, "How could America not care more for people? How could these people not care more for themselves?"

At that time a group was marching on Washington. To call national attention to their cause they set up a shack village along the mall between the Lincoln and Washington monuments. The city struggled to create sanitary facilities to keep the center of political America from becoming a cesspool. These crusaders either did not see or did not respect the beauty they occupied, and they did not see or care about the litter they created. They also did not know that they were creating a spiritual litter that was cluttering the very spirit their cause was urging. Bumper-to-bumper cars circled the mall as the dumbfounded motorists stared at this antithesis of beauty.

These seeds of insensitivity and a debased spirit are planted in almost every city in America. Citizen apathy can produce a cancer of ugliness in your own hometown. Take a drive around your community for an in-depth look. (Photos 17, 18.)

A major aspiration of this book is that we might heed President Spencer W. Kimball's plea to beautify our homes and communities. It is more than a call to tidy up. Most people can recognize raw ugliness with its loss of spirit. Fewer recognize

aesthetic litter and the loss of a higher spirit. This degrading
thief of spirit robs us of the strength that lifts us from mediocrity. Neither President Kimball nor any Church leader has ever
suggested that we be mediocre. The challenge has been to "be
perfect." Would a spiritual leader urge us to be perfect in all
things except good taste?

We all have much to learn. I know enough to affirm that
President Kimball is an awesome spiritual leader and that he
well knows the impact on Church members of living in beautiful surroundings. A highlight in my life was to drive with him
for several hours on our way to a conference. We talked art for
over an hour and I came to know firsthand of his giant stature
in sensitive things and of his desire that we live beautifully,
spiritually as well as physically. To live beautifully is a part of
character.

A community without a church reveals its character. The

Seattle City Light

17

design of a church building also reveals character. Our churches should be just as sensitively designed as any building we erect. The great cathedrals of Europe that can be studied in any art history book were built by people who lived in very modest houses. What their homes could not nourish spiritually was well provided by the cathedrals. Constructing great buildings creates spirit in the builders.

Award-winning architecture that is good enough to be included in a fine art history book gives evidence of sensitive design. Beyond that, it displays a design idea that is compatible with the spirit of those who will frequent that building. When Viktor Lowenfeld studied the homes, churches, and industrial buildings of America, he felt that the buildings were not compatible with the spirit of our lives. He wrote:

> Today, no one who has the choice of selecting an automobile would select an "outmoded" model. . . . Here we express a "taste" quite in

Seattle City Light

18

contradiction to the one which we expect in most of our homes. Are we then split personalities who accept different styles in different living areas, . . . streamlined simplicity in the kitchen, and complex patterns of ornamentation in our bedrooms? Why is it that the utilitarian areas of living have accepted our modern style, while our homes and social institutions still adhere to the past? Our medieval man could pray in churches full of spiritual and religious power, built in the most contemporary styles. The best . . . architects were chosen to design them. If one period changed, the style changed with its spirit. Today we pray in churches which mostly are poor imitations of times long past.

What is the reason for all these discrepancies in our modern social and cultural institutions? Apparently we have no confidence in these vital institutions, for if we felt the need to glorify them, the places that housed them would express this spirit. It seems that we have more confidence in our industrial power and institutions than in our religious forms. . . . This, however, is significant in itself, as it reveals a most serious threat toward our ethics and civilization, especially as this is underlined by the fact that the home and family life of today have seemingly to find refuge in past periods. (Lowenfeld, *Creative and Mental Growth*, pp. 40-41.)

Lowenfeld was not asking for our bedrooms to be duplicates of our kitchens. Each room of a house or an apartment has a different spirit that influences the functional as well as decorative design. In the same way, the various buildings of a community have their own functions and decoration. What Lowenfeld was suggesting is that when we design a home, a community, our personal effects, and especially our churches, if we do so without sensitivity to spirit and form, our senses will be jarred. What I am urging is that we do not live with either dead spirits or ugly ones, but that we search for the vital spiritual elements of our homes, churches, communities, and personal lives in order to foster a more sensitive environment that will in turn lift our sensitivities toward higher spiritual growth.

8
Hot Bread and Warm Neighbors

*The search for community spirit and
environmental aesthetic taste must be
found in the collective sensitivity of
warm neighbors and a public-spirited
citizenry.*

A magnifying glass big enough to see my whole hometown
was given to me by a man as I was leaving a class in graduate
school. I didn't see the lens in his words at first when he asked,
"You're from Brigham Young University, aren't you?"

When I gave an affirmative nod, he asked if he could talk to
me for a few minutes and he motioned us to some chairs. He
wanted to know some details about the university: what opportunities were open in teaching criminology, psychology, or
sociology at BYU, and what offices to contact for employment.
He mentioned a few details about his background, including
the fact that he was currently a prison psychologist in his home
state.

I outlined a few details about the school, which persons to contact and student-body composition, and I concluded with what I felt was a realistic statement that he should know: "Salaries at universities in our part of the country are lower than those at other schools such as . . ." Before I could reach the end of my sentence he said, "Who's talking about salaries? I'm talking about children."

I wondered how in the world I had missed anything he had said about children. His face was full of earnestness, and with words full of emotion he told me that his children were the most important part of his life and that he had not forgotten the first visit he had made to Provo. His visit convinced him that Provo was where he wanted his family to live, and it was the kind of place he dreamed of for his children to be in during their formative years. He said he would accept any sacrifice of salary—he felt it was imperative to move his children out of his part of the country because there were so many negative elements in his hometown. He knew BYU was a church-related university of a different faith than his own, but everything he had seen from the moment he had driven into Provo had told him that this was the place.

What elements did he see in Provo's environment to make him conclude that he should make any sacrifice for a community pattern? What made him decide that Provo had the power to influence his children in good directions? He was a qualified psychologist who could see in the community pattern the subtle elements he felt were so fundamental to a good life. As I talked with him it was apparent that the elements that attracted him were fused together in a total community spirit. Such a spirit interests businessmen because it affects the economy in dollars and cents; it interests church men because it affects eternal life.

When I look at the letters-to-the-editor column in any newspaper it is obvious that there are many kinds of communities with their personal spiritual characteristics. Some are like Provo; some are like the community of my psychologist classmate. Laguna Beach is known for its art, Las Vegas for its nightclubs, San Francisco for its Golden Gate, Portland for its high quality of life, Boston for etiquette, Pittsburgh for steel, Beverly Hills for its celebrities. Some of these attributes rise from natural resources; others are created from the lives of a kind of people. But most cities are multifaceted; any label is difficult to attach to them. Any neighborhood or suburb or town will still be what the people are. A way of thinking can become a way of living, and a way of thinking is influenced by community design. Pearl Harbor used the seabee slogan after the December 7 attack: "What is difficult we will do right now; what is impossible will take a little longer." Pearl Harbor workmen became identified with this slogan. In the war crisis, shipyard miracles were wrought. Communities can carry this same intensity of spirit.

"We're number one! We're number one!" This chant gets into the blood of enthusiastic rooters for an athletic team. When the sports polls declare that a certain school is rated first, there is a superior air that floats over the devoted fan. Athletes wear their letters with a bit more polish on their pride. When the past winners of the Super Bowl returned home, the hometowns exploded with uncontrolled spirit.

But when a young soldier comes home from a war he is probably not looking for the emblems of a Super Bowl winner. Every detail of his hometown has new meanings to him—main street's friendly crowds, the corner drugstore with its squeaky door, the grade school where he stuck his gum on the door jamb for pickup after school, the old movie house, a rusty nail almost buried in a branch of a tree that once held a rickety tree house, the garage where his uncle let him tear down his first engine, the library with a reproduction of Turner's "Snowstorm at Sea" that held his vision in the painting's storm. The emotional side of spirit makes coming home one of the great human experiences. Too often we let these details of spirit be a matter of chance.

What the prison psychologist sees when he drives into town

and what a young soldier sees coming home from war may be two markedly different things. One witnesses the signs of a community character, the other finds points of identification that warms his nostalgic spirits. A mother sees the town's influence on her children in a different way than her children see the potentials for entertainment. Communities are not static things; they are alive, and they give release to many kinds of spirit.

With teamwork we can make of a community what we want; a community, sometimes without our knowing, can make of us what it is.

A town without a church will be a different town than one with many churches. A town with several empty churches will have a different spirit than a town with a single church that has people packed from door to pulpit. A town searching for sensitive things surely will contrast with a town of taverns. A designer who won my highest respect wrote, "If we do not guard against unwholesomeness, it grows up about us and seems to become functional, or at least strongly habitual." (Neutra, *Survival Through Design*, p. 110.)

Also, a business community without homes radiates a different kind of spirit than a commuter community where the business employees return from work to be with their families. As soon as we create commercial centers separated from residential areas we declare a functional design.

In most European cities the shopkeeper lives above or behind his store. A European with a love for fresh bread simply walks a few steps and he can be at a neighborhood bakery, whether he lives downtown or in the suburbs. Each day the family shopper goes to the fruit market, to the vegetable stand, or to the butcher, all within his immediate neighborhood. A BYU student from Yugoslavia who has enjoyed this market lifestyle says he is unable to see any reason for the strange custom in America of shopping once a week and of making the home a store! In Europe there is a friendliness in knowing each of the merchants and talking with neighbors and workers along the way. But today the American word *supermarket* has been raised over many European stores. Supermarkets signal cheaper prices and a greater variety made possible through mass production; prices and variety pull people from more distant neighborhoods to shop with strangers. Supermarket shopping has a different spirit than neighborhood marketing.

Obviously each neighborhood cannot have a steel mill with workers living upstairs. For us to have the advantages of steel, workers are forced to travel. Businesses with heavy equipment have accepted the trend toward expediency by moving nearer the railroad tracks, manufacturers nearer to coal fields or power sources, government offices into complexes, financial institutions into proximity with each other. In agriculture, soaring food prices have demanded larger farm machines to handle greater volumes at less cost. Students who most lament these dehumanizing trends often travel to universities that specialize in their favorite subjects.

If commerce can so dramatically manipulate us to meet its needs, people should be able to design communities to meet people's needs.

The idea of a row of neighborhood shops has not completely died in America. Many communities now have designed shopping malls including an aesthetic atmosphere within, (photos 19, 20) although some mall builders have jumped into the business so quickly that they have created visual chaos. Some residential areas near mall construction have homes nestled in beautiful surroundings that nurture children's aesthetic outlooks.

Industry has changed the face of the neighborhood; malls and freeways have changed the face of America. Such massive changes as these affect our spiritual lives. We cannot afford to be ignorant or complacent.

As our communities have become specialized and as people have been forced to travel farther to work, we have created one of our spirit shredders: the hectic five o'clock rush. The feelings that once connected work and living have been stretched so

19

20

thin that many have snapped. I was leaving an office in New York's World Trade Building when the rush hour struck. Instantly the halls were flooded with people, and we were swept along to the elevators. Elbows and hot breath and hard words poked at our sides and senses. Huge elevators gulped in the masses and those left for the next bite lamented the discrimination. On the street an avalanche of me-firsters poured into the subway tunnels, which were covered with grubby graffiti. Glum, unhappy people seemed to resent their mole status. Perhaps many would rather return to the calmer days before the industrial revolution, when the baker lived behind his oven, the miller lived over his waterwheel, the farmer slept in the same building with his cattle, and warm neighbors offered extra hands for heavy tasks.

Spirit in a community or a neighborhood is more difficult to achieve in a congested, heavily populated community. The smaller the community, the warmer the neighbors. But a segment of a large city with families of like spirit can produce warm relationships. I am reminded of a neighborhood in Honolulu at the time Hawaii was attacked at Pearl Harbor. Emergency military law required all citizens to be off the streets by six o'clock. Movie fans had to be in the theaters by three in the afternoon for the final showing in order to catch the last bus home. Windows were "blacked out" with blankets or dark paper, for the city of Honolulu blew out all the candles in December 1941 in a wish for more security. Civil Defense joined the security movement and urged each family to dig an air-raid shelter.

In one part of Honolulu five or six houses surrounded a small open area. These neighbors were close church friends and they decided to build a neighborhood bomb shelter together. While some families dug with drudgery by themselves in their own yards, these friends made a party of it. They dug a large, multifamily shelter in the center of the joint land behind their homes. Everyone worked on the project, increasing their hooks of identification with each other. The sharing was fun, and the finished shelter was a proud achievement. Flowers were planted to top it off with a smile.

When night turned the city into a tomb and all public entertainment died, these neighbors came to life. Two or three times a week they would take turns hosting a potluck dinner, and the other neighbors would slip across the dark, open place, skirting their flower-decked bomb shelter to join neighbors at the host house. On a Sunday night they would organize a fireside to study a religious topic. Another night they would play family games or have a learning night about some issue of the war or about some topic of a group member's expertise. Their zest for life, the excitement of living together while the city buttoned lonely blackout robes, made such an impression on me that I was immediately converted to the quality of life that could be achieved with effective community design and primary experiences of identification.

My next-door neighbor saw these virtues many years ago, and as houses were built in a circle around a large open space in our neighborhood, he hoped the openness could be preserved and made available as a playground for children. He made a proposal to the owners of the property, and they were willing to let us use it without charge for five years with the option that if we maintained it attractively we could have it for a second five years.

The neighborhood project of preparing the land was a spirit builder in itself. After a bulldozer had leveled the ground, a big rake was attached to Uncle Bud's jeep. More weight was needed to keep the jeep's wheels from spinning and to hold down the rake for the final smoothing. Neighborhood children were delighted to provide the weight by jumping aboard. Around and around they went, dust and all, to make them feel a part of the park from the beginning. (Photo 21.) A sprinkling system was added, a lawn was planted, swings were added for the smaller children, and a basketball hoop was installed for the older youth.

The children that rode the jeep rake have now married and

moved away. As the years passed, more houses were built and more children used the park. The depth of belonging is not as keen for the new wave of children, nor do they care for the park as much. If we wish to teach caring we need to provide more identifications. One small identification was made when a neighbor suggested that, in appreciation of the Taylors, a sign should be placed on the park. The new children watched the ceremony of placing the sign saying "Uncle Bud's Park" in a way that gave them a link although it lacked the depth of the original primary experience. There is a difference between making something and enjoying something.

The enjoyment, however, has been a great part of our neighborhood. Children, youths, and adults have found the park a wonderful place for play and parties: potluck picnics to welcome neighbors, Frisbee frolics, Fourth of July events, and lots of sports activities. Parents and children playing volleyball with neighbors and then sitting down to loaded tables are building more than muscles and stomachs.

21

I think one of the most important parts of the park is the requirement for each family to take a turn cutting the lawn. This physical task is an inconvenience, but if city employees took care of these details important spirit identification would be lost. A father who hires the job done or does it by himself misses the chance to make the park "our park." The values of a family affair can multiply. The property owners sensed this, and in a neighborhood-minded spirit we have been able to complete over three five-year, no-cost leases. The property has become too valuable to remain in grass much longer, but while the grass has been growing, so has neighborhood spirit, and so have children.

A neighborhood without an area to make into a park can surely find some kind of an activity for growing community spirit. We can survive without a park, but when we stop caring about the little things that tie us to neighbors, children, and values, spirit is harder to find—and so is survival.

Among these little things we must care about is visual litter. Ugly signs, telephone poles, trash in empty lots, poorly designed buildings, and traffic patterns that jam intersections all contribute to a "Who cares?" feeling. Creating a beautiful way of living requires willing workers as well as sensitive people. Apathy is the greatest enemy to neighborhood design. Some may be sensitive enough to complain, but do we care enough to do something about it?

Rotterdam proved that no situation is hopeless. During the Nazi attack on Holland, Germany threatened to blow up a complete city block if the people would not bend to Nazi will. The Dutch spirit would not be bent—a Rotterdam block was reduced to rubble. A new Nazi demand met repeated resistance, and a second block was destroyed. The Dutch spirit held through the third, the tenth; Rotterdam was completely leveled.

After the war ended the determined spirit was still there and Rotterdam, once dead, rose from ruin to become one of the most alive, spirited cities of Europe. That vitality spilled into its design; new civic ideas were explored, new designs were created for traffic flow, and pedestrian walkways were designed with attractive visual interests such as plants, benches, and artworks. Even advertising signboards gave eye appeal. Other cities could not resist the example and they began to pull down buildings untouched by war. Old cities have a charm that is exciting to visit; Rotterdam has a spirit that is exciting to live in.

Warsaw also was leveled in World War II. The spirit of her people during the systematic destruction of their city was as intense as the Dutch spirit was in Rotterdam. Warsaw's spirit, however, was not given its freedom with the war's end, and an occupation to control thought was imposed from the East. Warsaw was rebuilt with Red fingers holding the strings of spirit. Fresh ideas in design were not tried. New buildings were made to look like old buildings. Design solutions to contemporary needs and functions were not incorporated. To look at the streets of Warsaw with sensitive eyes is a completely different experience than to view the streets of Rotterdam. Both design and spirit are still in bondage in Poland.

Bondage is not a monopoly of war. A little boy caught in the big city squeeze had to use a dirty alleyway near a European student center for his playground. Turning the corner to his play area one day we found a student standing quietly to one side watching the boy. Distress was written on her face as she said, "It's not fair. He doesn't have a chance." Other students passed as we watched. Our study of the boy drew their attention and they too shook their heads with an understanding of the drab, dirty surroundings of the child's play area and the limited perspectives he had.

Most of us can see the trash that blows on the sidewalks of our communities, but often we do not know the depth of more subtle visual and aesthetic litter any more than the child realized the dearth of his situation. This child's spirit was not under a Red thumb in Warsaw; it was held in bondage under a dirty thumb unwashed by community design.

Many of us stand in visual bondage under clean thumbs. Visual bondage is more than dirt. Do we know spiritual enemies? The enemy to our personal or community spirits is often a very subtle fellow. I discovered him in one of his guises while I was studying at graduate school, when some interesting statistics on highway design caught my attention. A man driving home from work without any speed restrictions who was required to break his speed at numerous stop signs would arrive home with his nerves on edge and would be more likely to speak sharply to his wife or children. If the man were held to a certain speed limit but had no interruptions on the freeway he could arrive home in good spirits. How we design even our highways makes a difference in the spirit of our homes and our communities.

One of the most important books I read during this time was Richard Neutra's *Survival Through Design*. He emphasizes that when a designer does anything for us, no matter what the means or materials, "he deals primarily with nervous systems and he caters to them." (P. 197.) Citing the millions of Americans in mental hospitals as evidence, he presents a strong case that much of our mental illness is not accidental. He says, "With our mammal lungs we might dive deep into water and survive for some minutes. It is true that man can expose himself to anomalous and unfavorable conditions and endure hours, weeks, years under strains of maladjustment. But the effects of improper environment are often cumulative, and we pay a penalty for spending long periods of our lives enmeshed and entangled in unnatural, abnormal surroundings, such as we now have to face every day." (Pp. 194-95.) Neutra's conviction that the number of people in mental hospitals is directly influenced by design irritants is based on his extensive examination of our social structure, psychological data, and aesthetic design. He explored the home, school, and civic patterns as well as a potpourri of environmental visual litter. We cannot ignore his conclusions or we may lose a desired quality of life or destroy our mental well-being.

However trivial any community concern may seem, I think Neutra is right: the patterns of our communities can build or destroy us, physically, psychologically, aesthetically, or spiritually. Many forces are bent on destroying community beauty, character, or spirit. We cannot be complacent about environmental design.

9
"His Taste Is All in His Mouth"

"Man has traditionally found expression
in music, poetry, painting, the per-
forming and plastic arts, in the sciences
and industrial technology. Only recently
has he begun to give this impulse
expression on a large scale in the art and
science of designing his environment."
Laurance S. Rockerfeller,
Chairman, White House Conference

The most devastating thing my brother-in-law can say about a man is, "His taste is all in his mouth." I hope I can wiggle out from under such a label of complete aesthetic insensitivity. The fact is that too many of us are content to live in mediocrity, and that many others do not seem to know that there is even such a thing as an aesthetic environment. Our homes and communities are ample evidence that much of our taste is in our mouths.

In 1851 Prince Albert of England devised the idea of hold-ing a World's Fair in London. His satisfaction with this popular success was marred by the glaring inferiority of British goods compared with goods from countries such as France. That in-feriority was exposed to the eyes of all the world.

The concerned heads of England were put together. They decided England would not produce anything of finer quality until English people could appreciate a finer product. Thus the idea of public education in the arts was born.

When the next World's Fair assembled the goods of various countries, French authorities became alarmed as they noted the rapid advance of English taste and design. The French initiated an investigation to ascertain the reasons for the English leap forward in aesthetic understandings, and they settled on two points: the English program was directed at raising the aesthetic level of the general public so that the public would insist on better quality, and potentially able artists were given increased opportunities to perform for more sophisticated audiences. An art program for the public was accordingly introduced into the French schools.

America was slower in recognizing aesthetic inferiorities, but eventually the movement for a greater appreciation of the arts crossed the Atlantic.

Pulling oneself up by his aesthetic bootstraps is usually an individual thing, but here whole nations were tugging at taste. The French were well aware that Paris was respected for her art sophistication, and French pride would not take a second-place position. Art was also a major economic concern: at least eleven major houses of *la haute couture* (Dior, Chanel, Lanvin, Balmain, Givenchy, Ricci, Heim, Cardin, Gres, Balencia, and Yves Saint-Laurent) were the taste-makers in the international world of fashion. Paris was also the home for a host of major painters that included the Impressionists and those of most of the modern movements. The Louvre is listed with the best art museums in the world. French architectural masters include Corbusier, and in 1909 the first performance of Diaghilev's

Ballets Russes was held in Paris. Parisians enthusiastically love their city of art and they do not wish to leave its future as the "Capital of Taste" to chance.

What are the unique qualities of our individual communities? Do we have the Parisian drive for enriching this uniqueness or for lifting community good taste?

Sadly, many American communities accept art objects of inferior taste not only for the home, but also for the community. One indication of a community's level of taste is in its public monuments. A monument can be both teacher and symbol.

Almost every Turkish hamlet, village, or city has a monument in the center of town. The theme of all these monuments is the same: to honor the national hero, Ataturk. A quick glance at these statues immediately reveals the character of the community members, the vitality of their spirits, the level of their taste. Some monuments are ambitiously heroic; others are sensitively artistic. One community was obviously stingy in constructing its monument while another wanted an ostentatious flair. Some are crude: one village has a poorly proportioned figure of the "Father of the Turks" cut from a piece of plywood, painted in unblended colors, and propped up by a single two-by-four that might collapse with a butterfly landing. The character or spirit of this community is there for all to see, and what the visitor sees is what the citizens live with day after day.

What does a stranger see when he visits our communities? Indianapolis has two huge monuments to war; Salt Lake City centers on the colonizer, Brigham Young; Paris lifts up her eyes to an engineering idea in the Eiffel Tower; London, the monarchy; Catholic cities symbolize with an obelisk the triumph of Christianity over the pagan world; a statue of Jefferson is surrounded by the words of great ideas in Washington — Washington ghettos have no monuments. Community character and taste stand on the same pedestals.

A wise course for community aesthetic standards is to have

open-juried competition for artists of potential art monuments. Any community, or any organization in the community planning a public monument, has nothing to lose with such a plan and has much to gain in quality by opening the commission to competition. The best jury of art experts that can be assembled should make the final selection. Jurors from out of the state are more likely to upgrade the quality than those who might award commissions to friends of the sponsoring organization. We live with monuments for a long time, and a thoughtful decision is worth all the time expended. Weak works tire with time.

Some publicity attended the unveiling of a monument recently at a Church site in one of our communities. One of the simple tests I use for sculpture is to close one eye and squint the other to see what the large, basic silhouette of the work reveals. In great sculpture an abstract and beautiful shape is revealed. I tried this easy test on this monument and it failed. The basic shape looked not unlike a potato sack. The sculptor had concentrated on subject matter and expression more than design. Unfortunately, too, the expression was a surface sentiment, not a deep spirit.

If we are to have Church-related artworks good enough to be in the sphere of the greatest spiritual environment, we need to first improve the taste of the Church membership, as Prince Albert planned for England, so that the lay people will insist on increasingly higher quality. We need to be more competitive in obtaining the finest selection of art available to represent the Church and the spirit of the Church. The same should be true of any institution in the community.

Making a quick evaluation of a city's spirit by observing the community's monuments on display could be misleading, but it does serve as a clue to a city's thinking, sensitivity, and direction. Among other clues should be the treatment and conservation of natural beauty. These sites do not need to be grand vistas, but even simple space can be Wordsworth's "Haunts of Ease."

As soon as we recognize that we are examining an "organism in its total environment" we are thinking in Frank Lloyd Wright's idea of "organic design" mentioned earlier. Every part of our environment reflects community taste.

We evidently care so little for environmental attractiveness that a Presidential report noted that it costs over a half billion dollars annually to remove litter. In New York alone, $10,500,000 is spent annually to clean parks and beaches of the refuse that Americans thoughtlessly leave behind. (Photo 22.) Three million tons of refuse are dumped each year into San Francisco Bay.

Peter Blake says in his book *God's Own Junkyard* that Americans accept decay and blight without a ripple of concern. He believes that we are so money-oriented that if oil were discovered under St. Patrick's cathedral an oil well would be put in the center of the building. With that despair he verbally and visually packs his publication with examples of the visual pollution that has made America a junkyard.

Writers at UCLA agree with Blake's hypothesis about American apathy. They show that laws are relatively easy to

22

pass but difficult to enforce because so few people place public interest in front of personal gain. Without spirit, nothing can live.

Civic design starts with the community's needs and a spirited citizenry. Civic design must include the individual's felt needs; community needs for space, convenience, and efficiency; subtle psychological and physiological needs that have to do with health, mental well-being, and a strong moral climate. Then this organic view of design must be blended with artistic vision and aesthetics.

In our compartmentalized world many communities give little thought to the design that should link the community's various segments. Placing a glue factory in the midst of a family neighborhood or a saloon next to a church are extreme examples, but we too often do place areas next to each other that have conflicts in function. To prevent these unfortunate mixtures, men and women of vision and taste have worked to establish land-use plans and zoning ordinances. Newspaper coverage of zoning conflicts indicates that the idea of a designed environment does not yet have wide community approval. But without these instruments, the community often turns over the best farming land to residential development and then when the increased population needs more food, the poor land is pressed into agricultural service. Design touches our stomachs and purses as well as our aesthetic taste; we need to recognize that a painting or a community with elements randomly placed usually fails to have compositional unity.

Neutra felt one of the first civic designers worth applauding was the Mormon leader Joseph Smith, followed by Brigham Young. He wrote: "*Joseph Smith is the first, inspired, self*-taught *community builder* . . . to create a human social setting. . . . One cannot think of any greater challenging contrast than that between the Mormon foundations and what surrounded them in the makeshift disorder of pioneer days, the shapelessness of unskilled design, only here and there mitigated by thoughtless importation.

"I have again and again admired Brigham Young's almost miraculous continuation of this tradition after a revival from disaster. . . .

"Not even George Washington, although he used L'Enfant for a pitifully brief nine months, to leave some impression of planning in this country, compares with the indigenous, originally creative community design gifts of Joseph Smith and Brigham Young, who, in fact, stand lonely in the far-flung American scene, where no native, non-colonial, non-imported community expression has ever been found again." (Neutra, "The Mormons and the American Community," *Improvement Era*, Feb. 1960, pp. 112-13.)

The key ingredient of a community is its spirit. These pioneer leaders affirmed that not even the multiplication tables should be taught without spirit. Although a civic designer may plan for this subtle element, it must still remain a citizen responsibility. If we all go our own way with our own interests, community hash may be our end product. To keep the things we most cherish, we must accept that there is a public good where we sacrifice some of our self-interests. Part of our self-interest is time. More of our citizenry need to take the time to become better acquainted with aesthetic design. All the plans for efficiency and convenience created by a civic designer must be carried out in a community environment. We should support good designers who foster community development with a taste for the beautiful, who preserve natural beauty without inappropriate elements encroaching on these sites, and who are willing to sweat, if necessary, to prevent unsightly development.

A national art conference several years ago reported that some designers and social workers got together to devise a plan for a prison where all incoming prisoners were placed in large, unpainted cement cells, dormitory style. Their food was adequate, but of the simplest fare. No prisoner was required to work, but those who did received credit for the amount and quality of the work completed. With this credit they could acquire better food, a cell with more privacy, paint or pictures for the walls, or other improvements for their environment. A room with a cheerful primrose yellow paint was evidently worth the work, and almost all the prisoners were soon engaged in developmental activities. With the paint and better living conditions the spirits of the men rose; although all prisoners did not become model citizens, the differences in attitude and spirit were positive enough to attract our attention.

A prison is a community that has only a few variables to design; a city requires a very complex design. A spirited citizenry and competent civic designers can add primrose yellow to our community plans with aesthetic taste, and if we work to make those plans succeed, the spirit and growth of our hometowns will shine through all of their citizens—children, youth, and adults.

Part IV
The House of Highest Spirit

10

Symbols and Spiritual Security

The prime spiritual source of a com-
munity is its religious environment. Since
the time of the early Christians,
symbols have been used in Christianity
as identification links with spiritual
things. A person may also be a symbol.
Symbols can be powerful tools in lifting
our lives.

Climbing over and around the huge stone lions on the steps of the Utah State Capitol was a delight to me as a child and much more meaningful than seeing all the rest of the building.

When childhood passed and the lions no longer had "climb-ability" interest, I began to wonder what lions had to do with the capitol building anyway. Then I discovered books that pictured lions in front of castles and palaces. Some thrones of kings were designed in lion shapes. When Richard the Lion-

Hearted led his knights, his banners carried three lions; those lions are still on the British royal standard. The most monumental of all symbolic lions is the great sphinx—a lion with a man's head—in front of Egypt's pyramids. Tourists come great distances to view the sphinx. Time has stamped it with significance. What does it mean?

The lion has long been a symbol of royal power. Through the centuries the animal with the massive mane and thundering roar has been known as "the king of beasts." Anciently it was believed that a king or a pharaoh actually received spiritual power from association with lion symbols. And, of course, in battle men of weak spirit could rally more enthusiastically around a banner of the Lion King than around a battle flag of a goose.

The Christians gave the symbol of the lion to Mark. He was said to have been buried at Venice, and over the Cathedral of Saint Mark (as well as on almost all symbols of Venice) is a winged lion. The lions carved over the portals of the medieval cathedrals of France also refer to Mark.

The Jews were looking for the Messiah to come as a powerful avenger, but he came as a lamb—something that was difficult for a people in bondage to accept. A lamb does not have a chance against a lion. How could a lamb be the "King of kings"? But a new kingdom was coming in which the meek would inherit the earth, and this message of meekness could not be delivered from the Mount of the Beatitudes with the roar of a lion.

The Christian message of love, patience, service to others, and observance of the spiritual essence of the commandments was a new idea. It needed new symbols.

A symbol, by dictionary definition, is a "visible sign of something invisible, as an idea." Christian artists began almost immediately to find visual symbols for Christian ideas. Jesus had referred to himself as a lamb or a shepherd. One of the great painters, Van Eyck, created a masterpiece, "The Adoration of the Lamb," which now hangs in the cathedral at Ghent,

Belgium. The painting is loaded with symbols, and as people studied the painting, many ideas were communicated to them through these symbols. Christian artists were symbol creators.

Simple as the Christian message was intended to be, the number of symbols used in the early Church was extensive. When membership in the Church under Roman bondage placed life in jeopardy, identification with strangers was sometimes given by scratching a symbol into the ground to represent a fish. Jesus had called for fishers of men, but the symbol also represented Jesus and his divine heritage. Just as we use the word *NASA* as an abbreviation for the National Aeronautic and Space Administration, the early Christians used each letter of the word for fish—*ichthus*—to mean Jesus Christ, Son of God, Savior.

Scratched on many tombs of the early Christians was an anchor, the symbol of hope. This may be a harder identification for some, but I cannot forget when as a child my father took me to Fish Lake. In those days the lake was said to be so deep no one had ever been able to measure the bottom. Dad put me in a boat to fish while he went on down the shore fly-fishing. I can still remember the stark fear of sitting over that bottomless chasm with only a thin wooden layer of boat between me and the depths.

I looked less at my fishing line that day than I did at the rope that was tied to the bow of my boat as I floated ten feet offshore. My eyes followed the rope across the water to the anchor that was stuck into the mud at the water's edge. I saw the anchor as my only hope of survival against floating away into the lake and floundering into oblivion.

Decades later, only one glance at an anchor scratched by an ancient Christian on a tomb in the Roman catacombs was enough to tie me to their fears and hopes. Symbols can have great intensity, depending upon the amount of identification we have with them.

The Christian cross became a major symbol. The Latin Cross ☦ in Italy, the Greek Cross ☩ at Constantinople representing the four wounds in the hands and feet, the Maltese Cross ⳾ with its eight points of the Beatitudes, the Tau Cross, ⊤ which was likely the cross used for the prisoners flanking the Christ, the Celtic Cross, ⊕ which was intended to look forward to the risen Christ instead of back to the tragic moment, the Botonee Cross ⳾ with knobs or buttons to hold in the design edges, the Jerusalem Cross, and the Twisted Cross 卍 are some of the variations of this symbol. The crusaders carried the cross on their tunics; Joan of Arc carried her cross against the English; churches lifted their crosses to heaven on their towers.

The design of the cross was so effectively used that many Christians overidentified with the symbol until it was no longer a tangible expression of an abstract idea, but had become the idea itself. It was kissed with affection, bowed to in reverence, and prayed to as God. The cross was no longer a symbol, but an idol. That people could go so far in their identifications indicates the great power of symbols.

The beasts of evil also know well the power of symbols. They are not toothless lions. Christians who err in kissing Christian symbols in worship are at least thinking in Christian themes. Those who kiss the symbols of evil are so deeply anchored to the bottom of evil depths that their rescue will not be easy.

The Christians were able to make the symbol of a lamb stronger than that of the king of beasts. We are designing symbols for our day and for our unique environment. The beasts we face today can be met with simple symbols that can overpower any force if they are linked to the spiritual Master.

The first step in the search for sensitivity and spirit in a church environment must be a search into the awareness of each person. That step is needed to find a symbolic link with the abstract elements of this environment. Unless the spiritual link is made we may be nothing more than "sounding brass or a tinkling cymbal." One way to identify us with the Master of spirit is to search within the church environment for a symbol we can grasp that has meaning and that can lead us to new symbols.

Among the segments that make up a church environment are the teachers and officers, the members, the priesthood and auxiliary programs, the nature of the meetings, and the various parts of the worship services, including ordinances such as the sacrament.

A young man by the name of Lewis reached through this environment in my life and tied my spirit to almost every one of these parts. He did this seemingly complex task so quietly and easily that years were to pass before I became fully aware of how deeply I was tied to significant symbols. I might never have become aware of this subtle but sure spiritual linking that was made within me if it had not been for one of the emotional climaxes of my life.

My awakening came with a stunning letter I received from my wife during World War II. I could not believe the newspaper clipping she enclosed about one of my closest friends, Lewis. That was the night I suddenly realized what an impact Lewis and the Church environment had made upon my life.

Lewis and I had gone through public schools and Boy Scouts together; we had played basketball in the Church gym and we had acted together in the ward plays. We had often walked home from school together and talked about the future.

When we were university students and we met theological problems in our classwork we would drop into his father's home office. I thought Lewis's father was a stern man. As we talked, he would say, "Lewis, you are not listening." I would look quickly at Lewis, and it always looked to me like he was listening; at least his eyes were open. Disciplined responses were expected, and Lewis quickly obeyed. The answers to our questions were always given in black-and-white clarity; his father saw no gray areas. I thought Lewis's father loved a correct answer more than he loved his son.

Eventually Lewis left on a mission, and a year later I left on mine. When he returned the war was being fought and he went into military service. After my mission was completed, I too enlisted in the service.

Overseas at my base in India I was examining some navigational charts ready for the printing presses when I became aware of a figure watching me from the doorway of the drawing rooms. It was Lewis!

I had not seen anyone from home for many months, and seeing Lewis appear out of nowhere was like someone had lighted a case full of fireworks. Almost five years had separated us, and somehow hitting him on the shoulder with my fist seemed to confirm that this was all real. His bigger fist hit me back with even more power, and the thump made me know how real it was. Seeing Lewis was a greater treat than seeing the Taj Mahal.

Lewis was important enough to me that I requested a duty release, and we walked back to my quarters talking without paragraphs. For more than fifteen hours we talked, taking time off only for dinner. We talked mostly of home, friends, and post-war hopes. Lewis also told me a bit about his military work in counterespionage. I cannot think of a time in my life when I had a longer conversation with anyone than I had with Lewis in the Indian village of Khragpur.

The next morning I went down to the airbase to say goodbye to Lewis. He was willing to pose for a photograph by his airplane, and then he disappeared into the sky. India seemed more lonely than ever before.

I wrote a long letter to my wife that night telling her about the visit and about what a tonic it had been for me to see Lewis after so many years. His visit was the greatest event of my overseas experiences.

When Jeanne received the letter, she read it and was just slipping it back into its envelope when she heard the newspaper boy bang the paper against the front door. As she went to the door and picked up the newspaper, one item seemed to leap from the page: Lewis had been killed in a plane crash on the flight back to his base in Africa.

When I received the news from her I was devastated. It was the first time one of my friends had died, and Lewis was at the core of my childhood. I realized that I had been the last one of any who knew him to see him alive. I did not want to talk to anybody; even the dinner call didn't interest me. As the men left for the dining hall I returned to my tent and, pulling out the photograph I had taken of him—his last—I leaned the picture against the head of my bed.

I do not know how long I stared at the photograph, but I was experiencing an instant replay of our long conversation, rapidly linking in a new train of thoughts. For the first time I realized how much Lewis had been building into my life. I could learn no wrong in his company. I had never heard him use foul language; he had never hinted of anything immoral; to him Sunday was a holy day. Lewis had always been Lewis; now I began to see him as one of the finest, cleanest young men I had ever known.

As I sat on my army cot staring at the photograph of my friend, I had to admit that Lewis had been a wall to many temptations I might have slipped into had I lacked his screen of protection. He had been an anchor; now he was a symbol.

All through the years I had been tying cords of identification with the Church and had not realized, until I sat on an

23

army cot with a picture of Lewis, that the Church environment itself had become probably the most significant symbol of my youth. I had never really known that I owed a thank-you to a church building. It had always just been there. On one side of the foyer was the chapel where we had sung Church hymns under the dynamic leadership of a man who made singing fun; Creed Haymond, the Olympic athlete, had talked to us about the Word of Wisdom from the pulpit, and there were other favorite speakers.

On the other side of the foyer was the cultural hall. This was where we played basketball and created our plays. I cannot forget the roadshow where I was the wind, whistling and howling from the wings. Our scenery, over which I had labored with brushes of amateur anguish, was hauled in open trucks through the night as we dashed from church to church to stage our production. Many other social events, like dances, were held in the cultural hall. In the field by the church we had taken our scout tests and had eaten huge amounts of barbecue. Those were all great anchors.

A church structure must be more than a design for worship. The spirit that pulls youth together into church activity is a product of three things: the design of the structure, the warmth of the spirit abiding in and shared among the members, and the worthiness of the members that enables them to attract a divine spirit. These are abstract ideas, but through these abstractions the church structure becomes a tangible symbol.

Counting my youthful blessings, focused by a tragic death, I found myself pouring out some of my feelings about Lewis in a long letter to his father. I bore testimony of the good life of his son and of his contribution to my life. The long conversation Lewis and I had had was also part of my letter, and I enclosed the last photograph.

By return mail I received a letter from Lewis's father. The preceding two weeks had not eased my distress, and I felt the letter was something I should read in a quiet place. (The search for a quiet place itself was an inspiration.) In remembering my visits to Lewis's father's office and remembering his to-the-point answers that sometimes felt a bit cold, I expected the letter to be a short note. I was wrong; it was a long letter.

I was also wrong in my cursory judgment of the father's feeling for his son. In simple, direct words the letter was an outpouring of a long-abiding love for Lewis that convinced me instantly that I had misread the signals. Any son could feel forever secure to have a testament from his father like the one I was reading. He also gave his own witness of Lewis's fine life and thanked me for my confirmation.

Then this great father, who had never been overcome by any temptation, who had never let the gray areas enter his life, wrote that Lewis was so important to him that he would give extra guard to his life to insure that he would be with Lewis in the eternities—for he knew Lewis had received the highest eternal achievements. He then bore his testimony of the truthfulness of the gospel to emphasize his point. At the bottom of the letter I looked at the father's familiar signature: "Joseph Fielding Smith."

I had always respected Joseph Fielding Smith's strength of character and leadership, his dedication to the Church and its principles; I had listened to scores of his sermons, had sat in his office with his son—and still I had not known the man. My growth was instantaneous. The next time I heard him speak I understood new dimensions in his sermon.

The letter I read in India from Lewis's father told me how much he cared, not only for his son, but for all sons. I suddenly saw that he had preached about righteousness not, as I had thought, because we simply *should* obey, but because he *cared* for our righteousness. I had never questioned that he was a prophet. I had simply missed his *caring* spirit of a prophet.

At the war's end I received a message that Lewis's body had been returned home for burial. The casket's appearance stirred my thoughts of India to the last detail. The spirit of the man I admired was not in the box, but the physical presence was a part of a spiritual symbol to me and I had come to know that symbols are powerful tools. They may be lowered into graves, but effective symbols can never be hidden. For twenty years I worked with the youth programs of the Church, and Lewis was a constant symbol before me in all those years. My objectives centered on linking youth with spiritual things through the symbols of an actual church structure and with programs that met their needs, including a philosophy of hope and security.

Some youth and some symbols today have reached higher than ever before. Some youth and some symbols have skidded to depths that could hardly be imagined by youth in my teen years. Symbols against the standards of the Church can be seen in newspapers where the chinks in the moral fortress have turned into chasms.

Those of us who feel that the Church is an armor against the barrage of negative stimuli must still find a way to put the child or adult inside its protection. It will not happen by chance or without effort, without strategy. The pulpit can meet the spiritual needs of many, but even the Christ was not able to awaken all people. And the Savior did not charge us simply to try to reach *some* people; he said *every* soul had value. Identifications with symbols are a part of the armor.

Through the years it has seemed to me that those who do not tune to spiritual tones as quickly as others are persons who have not achieved or met three primary things: a sensitive personal awareness, a setting that lifts rather than disturbs the senses, and primary spiritual experiences in religious involvement. A scientist with a symbol of man's welfare before him, a long caring for sensitive things in refining a personal awareness, an atmosphere to vitalize his search rather than distract, and a primary experience with things of the spirit may win more important achievements than the Nobel prize.

The physical church structure, the programs within, the Lewis Smiths, and the other elements of the Church environment are primary symbols needing sensitive attention. The symbols we create and identify with are important guides in our eternal voyage to sensitivity and spirit.

11
Holes in Our Holiness

Some of my most enjoyable moments of attending church as a youth were spent hearing Alma Selander play the organ. When possible I sat where I could watch his hands coax out the chords. I became so organ-oriented that when a new organ was being installed in our chapel the event captured all my spare time. Watching its creation from over the workmen's shoulders, I willingly volunteered to serve the installers as a pipe carrier or a parts passer.

The night of the first performance I was sure the most beautiful music in the world came from that organ. Because I felt a part of the instrument, the sounds ran up and down my spine as well as up and down the keyboard.

It was a disaster to me when Church leaders announced that there should be no music during the sacrament. I was very distressed. The silence during the sacrament seeped into me until I felt completely empty. It dramatized even more how much I had enjoyed the organ. The reasons for the decision must have been given from the pulpit, but my identifications with the music were so strong that the reasons could not penetrate my consciousness.

Eventually it dawned on me that with all my appreciations I had not been appreciating the major reason for attending church. Thoughts of the sacrament and its significance had been lost in my admirations for a fine organist and for great composers. An important step in my life came when I willingly set aside my reverie with a pipe organ during the sacrament in order to accept the wisdom of church leaders and to subsequently catch a new awareness of the sacrament service. Two things had happened to me: I had discovered that even good influences could block important spiritual experiences, and I had learned that I needed to listen with a more open mind to those with richer experiences, be they church leaders or leaders in any field.

If a beautiful organ can block full participation in a sacrament service, I wonder how many other kinds of blocks we might be building in front of our vision, such as the visual clutter in the foyers of churches. The sacrament is one of the most sacred of Christian symbols. If we fail to provide identification with the symbol, if we fail to screen out detracting elements, we should not be surprised if a reverent attitude is not achieved.

During most sacrament services many members will be in thoughtful postures, but the eyes and actions of others are not too convincing of deep worship. During one sacrament service I heard a teenager in front of me counting the folds in the window drapery; he whispered to his friend that there were more folds in the third drape than in the first two. A lady near me was making a grocery list for Monday; her daughter was watching the list being made more than she was watching the administration of the sacrament. My thoughts weren't on the sacrament either, as I listened to and watched them both.

Distractions can snatch our attention as quickly as a frog's tongue snatches a fly. Each part of the church environment has

its grabber: curtains and all the decorative elements, our neighbors, the bench we sit on, a child who has slipped from a
parent's lap to stand with finger poised over the piano keyboard
as the speaker is about to emphasize his key point, indeed,
anything around us.

Obviously these elements can be either negative or positive.
Design elements can be made in a naive way by a person with
limited experience, or they can be made by a sensitive designer
of wide experience. Because we gather so many impressions
through our eyes, poor visual design can be a greater detractor
than music, especially when music can be turned off during the
sacrament while the visual detractors remain.

A special feature of good design is that attention can be
focused on whatever element the informed designer wishes;
advertising agencies know this well. Design may not capture
everyone's attention. Minds too filled with outside stimuli are
difficult to focus, but a mind prepared to worship can be
focused and a fluid mind can be nudged.

Using design to aid concentration on the sacrament is not
disrespectful. We naturally give our greatest design interest to
that which we most value. When critics felt that the Greek
artist was putting too much care on the carvings in the
shadowy corners of the temple, and that no one would be able
to see such details, the sculptor simply replied, "The gods can
see." The critics eventually learned to see with the gods.

Our attention can be attracted by things with "caring"
looks. Music is not a detractor when the congregation stands to
sing a hymn midway through a long meeting. Such a hymn is
designed more for mental and physical refreshment than to win
a music award, but if we were to care as much as the Greek
artisans we would make sure that the music chosen would lift or
tune our finest senses.

Finer senses are senses more ready for worship.

Of course, music and art are not essential for a worship
service. In a hotel room in Moscow a Russian girl attended our
sacrament service. With great respect in her attitude she com-

mented after the meeting, "The speakers were so sincere; the people I talk to in Russia aren't sincere." A beautiful spirit filled that hotel room and the sacrament was taken with great reverence.

But often we have holes in our holiness. I can't forget a trip I took across the United States and the churches I visited along the way. There were many things easy for a stranger to note. Often the foyers were simple illustrations of an insensitive introduction to a sacrament meeting.

In the foyer of one church we were greeted with a sign advertising an important youth gathering. The awkward lettering was made either by a beginner or someone who didn't care. Other posters were hung in the entrance way with a "pin-the-tail-on-the-donkey" approach. A chart by a better craftsman lauded the achievements of each Boy Scout in the ward troop; another chart gave attendance statistics for various organizations; a sign listed temple days and welfare assignments; and an idea popular in many wards, "The Family of the Week," was displayed with pictures and text on a clumsy easel. To top all of this off was a final sign that said, "Please be quiet, the other ward is in session." The reverence sign was lost in visual confusion. Here was an entrance to a worship service that had the touch of a carnival. Even more disturbing to me than the number of tacked-on posters was their chaotic arrangement. (Photo 24.)

We entered another meetinghouse with some visitors who were investigating the Church. The extremely naive display of covered wagons and pioneer materials for the Twenty-fourth of July commemoration was embarrassing. I noticed the visitors smile at each other, suggesting that our belief had not made us very sensitive.

Another investigator told me that when he attended his first worship service he thought he was entering a fieldhouse because he saw the prominent display of athletic trophies near the front door. (Athletic trophies are one of the ways a youth identifies himself with the Church or a program. A trophy in the basement does not create as strong a hook as in the foyer. Trophies need to be seen—the design question is, where?)

One church had a foyer that was completely bare—nothing at all. I felt like some kind of an inmate with orderlies who did not care.

Very few posters, charts, trophies, displays, announcements, and other foyer accumulations lack importance. They are placed for good reasons, but for spiritual worship we need the highest spiritual care, not visual litter. Right ideas must be aesthetically right if the perfection we are scripturally charged with is to be achieved. The design problems of a foyer are to be solved, not necessarily erased.

If the entrance to a church building has a "cared-for" look as the first impression, we are on the right track. Flowers are sometimes placed in the chapel by a thoughtful Church member, and they give a lively sparkle of color to make the meeting a happy, pleasant event. Flowers give the foyer a "someone cares" touch. It is impossible for one to care and not

24

have a worshipful spirit. Those who care can lead others to care, and a worshipful spirit has been increased.

Ward members coming to worship on Sunday should have a transitional development of spirit from the entrance to the chapel. As important as posters are, most of them do not contribute to a spirit of worship. Perhaps a better place to display announcements might be on walls or areas that are primarily seen as the congregation leaves the building. The posters would then be a last-minute reminder at the end of the meeting. But again, they should not be so strong that the sermon or lesson of the past hour is diminished.

Existing foyers are not likely to have wall-remodeling possibilities, but other things can be done. An obvious first step is to have every element—poster, trophy, floral decoration, furniture, or painting—be a worthy object in itself. Each should be well made, with a distinct sense of caring, and each should be aesthetically pleasing. If any decoration considered for the foyer is questionable on these criteria, it should be left out.

Second, the amount of attention each item pulls should be considered. Obviously a banner hung across the door to the chapel advertising a chuck-wagon dinner for the scouts would not be conducive to a chapel worship spirit. On the other hand, a typewritten notice might be too small to be seen by boys who have trouble standing still long enough to read small print. Members of a group promoting a certain activity may feel that their poster could never be large enough, but excess in any direction is in poor taste.

As one develops an identification with any object, there is a tendency to increase its decorative elements to the point of excess. The more elements in a design, the more difficult it becomes to keep all the elements unified. If the number of objects grows too large, even beautiful things will make visual litter. The visual field also becomes littered when miscellaneous items are displayed without any connection, artistic or psychological, to the primary theme.

Working with the visual problems of a foyer or some other

area of the religious environment could well be a specific assign-ment to a sensitive person. In many wards no one has received such an assignment. When selecting such a person, the appoint-ing leader should recognize that the crux of the assignment is the person's level of taste. The quality of the foyer design or other visual needs that are not a part of the original architec-ture will rise no higher than the person who is given the respon-sibility to raise that quality.

Sometimes a candidate for such a position may have been given local recognition as an artist for artworks that are in reality spiritually and aesthetically weak. A popular artist may not be a good artist. This may seem confusing, but it is a deli-cate matter. Stake or area leaders might make a critical search with carefully selected qualifying data to find the best aesthetic leader in the geographic stake area and to use his help in appointing and working with ward representatives.

Bishops and other church leaders are daily faced with many more critical problems than aesthetic ones. And yet a bishop knows as he sits counseling a youth that a very small thing can trigger some major behavior problems. Making a sensitive atmosphere for worship is an important assignment, and a coordinator with taste can relieve the bishop of his concern for the appearance of his ward or branch.

Because taste is such a confusing subject to many of us, and often such a personal thing, a ward leader may feel that a com-mittee can make a better judgment. Decisions involving color schemes, relationships of various items to each other, position-ing, and the spiritual tone of the building may be given a more harmonious feeling with a committee discussion. Appointing a youth to such a committee can help provide another identifying hook for the young person, and he in turn may bring other youth to a more sensitive care of the church structure and fur-nishings.

Another hole in our holiness came forcibly to my attention when I attended a national art conference. In the same city a church site with artwork was being opened to visitors, and some of the artists attending the conference went to see the work. When they returned to the art conference they were laughing about the quality of the art that was associated with religious ideas I held sacred. Their laughter has long been with me. From what I have studied about art I could see that their criticisms of the art were valid; I could not defend it. If they had criticized the Church I could easily have felt as Paul did—"I am not ashamed of the gospel . . ."—but I was ashamed of the quality of art. There was nothing I could say. I could only walk away.

For years I have felt like a deserter for walking away from those artists, and as they talked in the halls and over the dinner tables about the poor art of my church, I could not help but fervently wish that we had presented to the public a fine artwork that would have had them talking positively. Those artists never reached the religious ideas—poor art prevented any spiritual identifications.

This can happen to others besides artists. Religious concepts are enhanced in the atmosphere of fine art, and they are poorly represented by inferior art. We naturally expect missionaries representing the Church to be well groomed. Church presentations in the public community also need dignity and a high aesthetic taste.

No part of the church environment is unimportant. When the various parts—a human spirit, an art spirit, and a church spirit—work together effectively, they can build upon each other to achieve desired effects. Fellowshipping, for example, is obviously part of a good church program. Fellowshipping simply means blending human spirits into a harmonious relationship. Sometimes informal clutter can be in the spirit of lighthearted friendship, but fellowshipping and foyer decorations should both blend with divine things. A church charged to be a "house of order" needs to play the whole orchestration without discord.

To achieve an identification hook with a church or a part of a church service, such as the sacrament, or to direct attention in a display is often a design problem. To preserve the spirit of sacred ordinances, architecture should meet more functional requirements than just protection from the elements. One requirement is to use the elements and principles of design to create the spirit of dignity and respect that the aesthetic qualities of art are capable of producing. Although there is much I may never understand, I have formed a rather firm conclusion that the arts in their highest sense are definitely a part of perfection.

Organizing our lives on a course for perfection must include the divine design of ordinances and covenants. Probably the most sacred moment in a Sunday worship service is during the sacrament. At this moment we should remember the life of a perfect man and recovenant to keep his commandments. We do this that we might "have his Spirit" to be with us.

We obviously must be spiritually tuned to fulfill this ordinance. It seems to me that every person who appreciates the sacrament must have a personal relationship with the Savior, or have grasped the lesson of a great teacher, or been influenced by a setting. Sometimes it might begin with a small incident when a child who has long admired an older boy begins to notice the careful and reverent attention the older boy gives to passing the sacrament. When young men prepare the sacrament as though they were at camp, it is quite evident that they are not thinking of the man of perfect design nor are they reaching for his spirit. The congregation in some measure will be influenced too.

One Sabbath in the Holy Land we were fortunate to have the Garden Tomb all to ourselves, and under the branch leadership we held a sacrament service in that sacred setting. It was a most impressive service although no great cathedral soared over our heads. I noticed that each person took the emblems with great reverence, and the spirit of the meeting was very penetrating. It was an experience that I suspect not one participant has forgotten. It was as close as I have ever been to a perfect worship service.

We could not carry the Garden back home with us, but we did carry its spirit, and I know it has made a difference in my participation in the sacrament meetings I have attended since.

The spiritual environment we build around us affects our sensitivity and spiritual awareness. If each member of the Church would make an increased effort to search for a level of sensitivity and spirit just one measure higher than his present awareness, I am confident that the spiritual power of the Church would increase.

12
More Than a Steeple

Symbols, ordinances, and rituals provide
identification with abstract and spiri-
tual concepts. The physical church
structure is a major influence on the
church membership in providing identifi-
cation. Poor design does not need to be
evil to create confusion. An evil snag can
pull well-woven material out of align-
ment; a true architectural loom gives
strength to the fabric.

The chancellor of the University of California was once criticized for spending so much money for a bell tower on the Berkley campus. He immediately responded by saying that if each student would lift up his eyes but once a day, it would be worth every stone, brick, and trowel of mortar placed into the structure.

Steeples have a similar importance. Since a steeple's function is less obvious than that of a broom closet or a coat-rack, budget makers may look twice at steeple costs as they scan the list of chapel needs. But a suggestion to save money by deleting the steeple from the architectural plans would likely be rejected by church officials and the membership as well. "It wouldn't look much like a church," we might retort. And it is true that steeples have become a most readily understood symbol of churches.

The early designers of steeples evidently wanted to create a transition between the physical bulk of the church structure and the spiritual realms of heaven. They reasoned that as our eyes would naturally follow the vertical line upward, the physical dimensions of the church would become slimmer until at the point of the steeple we would lose the physical for the spiritual. Christians who pray with the palms of the hands together, fingers pointing upward, also intend a spiritual transition.

A steeple, then, has an important meaning. All parts of a church structure should mean something, and those meanings must be linked to the members themselves. A steeple is more than brick and stone; a chapel is more than a steeple; and the spirituality within the chapel is more than the whole structure. We need to remember that architecture has a spirit, that design influences human spirituality.

A concern was raised years ago in the Church that a building's spirit could be a competitor with the sacrament service. Plans were approved for some chapels with low ceilings and a minimum amount of decoration in order to avoid the over-powering nature of such structures as the Gothic cathedrals. With the architectural spirit almost inactive, a congregation of extremely devoted Church members would find no interference of a non-divine spirit. With such a congregation, the meeting inwardly stirred a high spiritual nature uncontaminated by external physical stimuli.

However, not all Church members had arrived at this level of spiritual experience. To potential converts, children, or those with minimal testimonies, the less inspiring architecture provided negative visual stimuli, and the bridge to a higher spirituality was narrowed. They were more conscious of sounds bouncing off the lower ceiling, more constricted in feelings of space, and they may have felt an architectural indifference—as though the chapel had been made by people who did not care.

Those in authority were aware that a lack of architectural involvement produced negative spirits, and plans for Church architecture with more design vitality were subsequently approved.

To enter a church where the structure is more important than the events inside is to expose ourselves to poor design no matter how beautiful the building might appear. The design of any building must harmonize with the function of the structure. The business of a church is not merchandising but regenerating spirit. Hence a church must not look like a mercantile institution. Just as the facade of an art gallery must convey more spirituality than the front of a bank, a church structure must convey more spirituality than an art gallery. Church designs that emphasize surface show and rich decoration can derail a worshipful spirit.

Effective architecture prepares the congregation's attention for spiritual learning. But a congregation needs spiritual education too. Parents who teach their children the little song "I Am a Child of God" are trying to establish an identificational link with a spiritual concept. We also carry into church a bundle of material for the children to play with—coloring books, "quiet books," dolls, games, and cookies. The objective is to keep children quiet. I have popped many cookies into a child's mouth to keep him quiet, but I wonder if that child may be forming an identification hook that the chapel is a place to play or eat.

Children have difficulty sitting still, especially when the sermon has no points of connection with their interests. To have children sit like ramrods, arms folded and nothing at hand, during a church service with adults may leave impressions that the church is an oppressive place, even a place to hate.

There are better solutions than the single choice between a chapel as a place to play or a place to hate. The objective of having a child view the church as a place of reverence may begin with a primary experience to help the child identify with that reverence.

A group of Church members in Paris acquired property in a central section of the city. The new facility was not as luxurious or efficient as the former chapel near the Arch of Triumph. The division also meant that fewer people would be available for the new responsibilities because their former co-workers were developing their own new facilities at Courbevoie.

But a wonderful thing happened. It was easy to feel a new and growing spirit of vitality among these Saints. The children could sense this surge among their parents as they helped in the physical work necessary to prepare the structure for church services. One wall was knocked out to enlarge the chapel. Children helped pick up the broken plaster and other building litter, or washed the railings and ran errands. Working shoulder to shoulder with parents, church leaders, and friends, the children were forming links with the physical church and welding links with their fellow workers. Identification experiences like these prepare the mind and the spirit to hear messages from the pulpit and classroom more clearly.

These Parisians also made a resolve that I hope they have been able to keep: they resolved not to use the chapel for visiting with friends. These Church members loved to visit, and their resolve was made even more difficult by an agreement with residents of the neighboring buildings that shared the same entrance courtyard. Because the courtyard walls amplified sound, the neighborhood rule was made that there would be no talking or visiting in the court. With both chapel and courtyard screened from visiting, all that was left was a small foyer and the staircase. After church services the staircase became a tower of talk. The French naturally run their words together, and in this tight place they could not get the words through sideways. The air was electric. But what an impact this chain of events has had on the children as their parents moved with them from the parlez-place on the stairs into the quiet of a chapel of their own creation, silently shifting gears to a reverent attitude.

Another example of influencing children's behavior and identifying them with a building was called to my attention during a visit to an elementary school in northern California. The teacher had guided her children in creating a large rock mosaic from small stones available in the school area. After the children's interest in the project had been aroused, the rocks were collected and separated by color into different piles while other children experimented with various designs. The size was ambitious enough to permit many class members to participate in the project; probably an old door was used for the base. When the stones were glued into place the final result was so handsome that the children danced with delight. (Photo 25.) The placement of the huge artwork was made with ceremony and I suspect that parents and school leaders as well as other classes attended the unveiling. A major hall of the school was chosen for the hanging.

Then came the magic of identification. In the minds and hearts of the children the building had become more "our school." The part of their spirits now attached to the wall gave the building a new identification and cause to be cared for. School leaders said that the children's efforts to keep the school halls cleaner was almost automatic. The spirit in the classroom had become a togetherness as they studied their masterpiece with admiring eyes; learning had been given a boost.

Families ready for church on a Sunday morning may attend any of a variety of church buildings—big churches, small ones, expensively built chapels, or modestly made assembly halls. Architecture's most important impact on the spirits of a family has little to do with dollars and cents. The modest little chapel

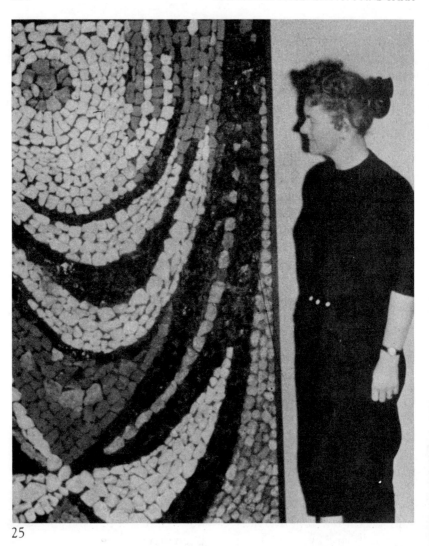

25

at Kalaupapa, Hawaii, pours out a magnificent spirit that seems to move every visitor who attends. The identification the members have with the building and the level of spirit come first. Church builders seeking a rich spiritual environment cannot buy this with money.

There is an interesting design phenomenon evident here: the belief a person holds, and the intensity of that belief, dictate the quality of design a person builds into the physical objects attending that belief. More simply stated, we place our greatest energy into the things we most believe. Wherever the heart lies, there is where we enrich design. Spiritual energy produced from the identification will be a melody that will linger, while decoration without depth becomes a "tinkling cymbal."

Seated at the back of a classroom of young teenagers, I once noticed a girl obviously not listening to the lesson. She was so wrapped up in her fourteen-year-old self it was hard not to notice her. Pulling a compact from her purse she snapped open a mirror and began to gaze at her reflection. She smoothed her eyebrows with the tip of a curved finger and studied the effect from a variety of positions in her mirror. Out came a lipstick tube; her lips tensed into a strange kind of a pucker as she painted her mouth. Tilting her head at various angles, she again studied her work. What she saw gave herself a vote of confidence and she turned her shoulders to a haughty angle of assurance. With utmost care she used a mascara brush to darken her eyelashes. Under a heavy load she blinked her beauty. Meanwhile, the lesson was progressing, but she was in a soundproof circle of love for her face. It was clearly evident that there was nothing in the world more important to her than her face.

This love affair was reflected in the design of an elaborate compact with extensive decorations and many compartments. One section held rouge, which she applied to her cheeks with a finger that moved like that of a person sorting unset cut diamonds on a velvet pad. A comb came out of the labyrinth of her purse and her hair received intricate attention. She was adjusting her earrings when she suddenly flicked her eyes into consciousness to discover that the class had ended and most of her classmates had left the room. With practiced dexterity the make-up materials dropped through red-nailed fingers into the perfumes of her purse. Evaluating once again the set of her hairdo with knowing fingers, she yawned, picked up a note-book too small to hold anything, and poise-peddled out of the room.

The girl with the painted face remains in my visual memory bank, not because of her attractiveness—indeed, she had so littered her face with superficiality there was no humanness to attract—but she has stuck as a prime example of one who would let preparation for life slip by in favor of goals of lesser importance. But whatever our evaluations may be of this teen-ager, she does illustrate that we tend to place our greatest decorative interests upon the things of most importance to us.

The cathedrals of Europe were the most involved, com-plicated structures of their times. The decorations and concepts of the buildings reveal medieval man's values as much as the girl's decorated face revealed hers. Medieval man believed in an "other world" society. Whatever his lot, if he were faithful through the trials and suffering of mortal life, he would merit a celestial world. Raising a church to God became his primary objective, indeed an obsession, and the face of Europe became covered with great cathedrals. The intense participation of the populace in the erection of the churches forged powerful hooks of identification of such strength that the church became the important force in their lives. Personal comfort, honor, posi-tion, let alone cosmetics, were gladly sacrificed for the construc-tion. Their devotion permitted long working hours and the architects gave more thought to a tiny detail on the drawing than to their own signatures on the plans. The architects and workmen so loved the Lord they seldom placed their names on the stones or the drawings. Their namelessness is a testimony of their spiritual beliefs. They built no veneers. They carved an identification with something outside themselves.

A church is indeed more than a steeple, more than beams and bricks and decoration inside and out. The spirit of the structure rises from the spirit of its congregation. The more that congregation identifies with each element of the design, the more spirit will be evident in the building.

Part V
Searching below the Skin of Beauty

13
Exploring a Pioneer Masterpiece

Spirit is often more easily seen in painting and sculpture than in architecture. Yet, paradoxically, we live more intimately with architecture than with the other visual arts. The need to build architectural identification in our children as well as ourselves has been stressed.

A certain pioneer architectural masterpiece is a vibrant example of spiritual involvement in a building.

Bones with wrinkled flesh hanging loosely from white knuckles reached out to me. I grasped the hand ever so gently for fear of breaking the fragile bones. As her fingers wrapped around my hand I could feel every joint. The ancient hand was light and it matched the thin voice that said almost without breath, "Aloha kakahiaka, Lunakahiko." I was standing in the presence of living history; she was over 100 years old, born before the first pioneers started the Oregon Trail to the northwest coast, before a house was built in the Intermountain West, before Lincoln ran for president, before her islands were discovered by English sailors. I was reluctant to leave her side, but others wanted to shake her hand and I had to make room.

Most people are not as eager to meet an old building. We can talk with old people, but we need to be quite sensitive if we wish to talk with an old building. When we talk with an aged person we can feel history made alive in the present; we can look directly into eyes that witnessed events of the past as they happened. And the same thing can happen with a piece of architecture. Those of us who are impressed in shaking hands with a live, 100-year-old hand can have the same thrill with a 100-year-old building—if the building was built with spirit and we have gained enough sensitivity to know it.

We need to know first that architecture is people; buildings are the products of human heads, hearts, and hands. If we learn to appreciate architecture we in turn learn to appreciate people.

One of the most important things my parents did for me was to teach me to walk in pioneer boots. They helped me to feel the ruts under pioneer feet walking across the plains, to feel the struggle of turning desert soil into food. I know I was changed as they helped me to live vicariously in others' lives and to walk into pioneer structures and touch the work of pioneer hands, to reach for the spirit of those departed hands.

Probably no early pioneer building in the West has more inner spirit left by pioneer hands than the Salt Lake Tabernacle in Salt Lake City, Utah. Few buildings have been more cared for, and it holds 100 years well—and with spirit. The flesh of the building's beams is not loose. Its bones are not brittle. They are proud bones, for they have held a roof of protection over great churchmen, over presidents of the United States, over the finest musicians to tour the nation. The building has no need to hide its face because of aesthetic mistakes. Its aesthetic spirit is a design masterpiece.

In 1847 the valley in which this pioneer masterpiece now stands was empty, a desert inhabited only by a dead salt lake. Then in July some pioneers pulled out of an eastern canyon. It was Saturday when the wagons rumbled down out of the foothills. Pioneer eyes swept the profiles of the mountains from the valley floor where they were to make their homes; they looked at the dry, hard ground where the families were expected to grow their crops, and the dust did not remind them of the fertile fields they had left behind in the East. The mammoth task ahead was to carve a living and to create a city.

The first morning in the valley was Sunday. Empire building would have to wait until Monday: this was a worship day. Obviously no single covered wagon could hold the company of pioneers, so they held their Sunday worship services in the open, dry field. Without shade the summer sun in the valley was uncomfortable, but pioneers were accustomed to being uncomfortable after a journey that spanned a barren desert and a craggy mountain range.

Pioneer leaders must have felt staggered by the tasks ahead. Crops and roofs were obvious firsts, but the Saints already wanted a place to meet for church services. During the first week some members from the Mormon Battalion arrived, bringing the total number of settlers to around four hundred. These men had just been released from their military service for the United States in the southwest, and Battalion muscle was put to work at once on the first building to be erected in the valley: a meetinghouse. Walls were made of poles hewn out of the mountain forest and hauled to the site, which had been selected as the center of the proposed city. Holes were dug for the poles, and leafy boughs were stretched from pole to pole to form a roof. By the second Sunday, church services were held in the comfort of the shade of this temporary bowery. The pioneer city in the desert was started with a place to hold church services; the beginning was a spiritual experience.

For three years while the pioneers were securing the necessities of life, cultivating their crops, building cabins for families, and constructing barns and pens for stock, the bowery had to serve their meeting hall needs. A second bowery with 100 supporting posts was made to meet the growing population. Community interest in a more permanent building was high, and a more substantial building that involved a year's labor was later constructed. Adobe was used to keep out both summer's heat and winter's cold. Trusses were used for the roof, making the hall free of the supporting poles that both cluttered the view and created barriers between speakers and listeners. Local needs were well met with this building, but at the next conference not all who came could crowd in. A few conferences later, when the leaders saw the throngs arriving seven thousand strong, they decided there was no choice but to meet outdoors as they had done the first Sunday in the valley. Another larger bowery was built.

Brigham Young, the man of vision who had led the pioneers on their historic search for a place of refuge, decided to build a permanent structure of greater size. As he talked with the Church leadership about his expectations they must have gasped. No building in the world had ever been built to meet his vision. He wanted it almost as big as a present-day football field, with no interior columns to support the roof—he was tired of visually and physically dodging all the bowery poles. What did the other leaders say to these ambitious dreams?

Perhaps they said, "No one has ever seen a building such as you envision. How could you make a roof that big?"

"How will the people hear in such a huge building?"

"How could a roof of over 37,000 square feet hold up under a heavy snowstorm? How could you heat it?"

"How could we get enough materials from the Missouri River docks with only ox-team wagons?"

"How can our people build another major structure with the temple already in progress?"

"It can't be done!"

These were small obstacles to a man who had already done impossible things. No man in his day had a more powerful spirit. Those with objections to the difficulties of the task must have felt a finger of his great spirit flip the problems aside and then, feeling the inspiration of that spirit, they too knew it could somehow be done. The plan was forming in Brigham Young's mind more than one hundred years ago for the magnificent Tabernacle.

An excellent historical record of the Tabernacle is *A Tabernacle in the Desert* by Dr. Stewart Grow. He records the building's most talked-about beginnings, including the story that Brigham Young took a boiled egg to a meeting, cracked it on the long axis, and after clearing out the egg, placed it on the table and said he wanted a building in that shape. Brigham Young's daughter said that her father got the idea from the elliptical shape at the back of the old adobe tabernacle, reasoning that if a band shell could make music more easily heard, the shape would do the same for speakers.

William H. Lund, former Church historian, said that when someone asked Brigham where he got the idea he replied, "From the best sounding board in the world, the roof of my mouth." Grow points out the interesting comparison of the teeth with the piers that support the Tabernacle roof when seen from outside. Another favorite story is that President Young snapped open an umbrella and asked for a roof built in that manner.

Dr. Grow concluded from his research, "It is unfortunate that the source of the idea cannot be proved; but regardless of the source, the important thing is that the architecture was both unique and successful." (*A Tabernacle in the Desert*, p. 96.) (Photo 26.)

What is conclusive is that the idea did not come out of the traditions of the past. Brigham Young did not search for solutions in old architecture books; he did not travel the world to see what the past had done with his problem; he did not call for an assembly of the best architectural minds from abroad. Here was a man of vision, and he and his own local architect initiated a procedure now used by the best modern architects: (1) they studied the functional needs, (2) they surveyed the contributing environment, (3) they examined local sources of materials, and (4) they designed an imaginative solution. Their efforts created an architectural masterpiece.

The Tabernacle has been considered one of the greatest architectural achievements in America. Any person who thinks of church architecture only in terms of Gothic cathedrals or magnificently carved decoration or even inspiring vertical lines (which are not found in the Tabernacle) may think that this statement is unrealistic. But the building deserves a second look.

If I were to venture my vote on the source of the idea I would say that perhaps Brigham had the egg, the umbrella, his mouth, and many other concepts stirring. Part of the background influence came when he stood in the boweries and

26

faced the congregation blocked from his vision by the hundreds
of poles holding the roof. He wanted to see their eyes; he felt
the poles were a psychological barrier. Those who knew
Brother Brigham wrote of his powerful spirit and his penetrating eyes. I am convinced that the bowery poles were a plague to
him. His voice could be heard, poles or no poles, but I am sure
that Brigham was so conscious of spirit that when his
projection had to wind around the poles it was visually and
spiritually disturbing to him. He wanted a direct communication.

Brigham Young contacted Henry Grow, the man who
would become his architect, and he visited Grow's lattice-
designed bridge crossing the valley river. The President must
have told the architect that he wanted a bridge big enough to
span a large congregation instead of a river, and then he
wanted to fill in the ends as a sounding shell. Grow caught the
vision, knowing it would take much skill and creativity on his
part to bring the idea to fruition.

The idea was fresh enough that the plans grew with the construction. In the conclusion of his book Stewart Grow states:

> The success of their efforts is made more remarkable by the fact
> that the building was erected with a minimum of over-all detail designed
> in advance of construction. As has been noted, the general plan for
> the walls and roof of the building, first announced in the Deseret News
> of 1863, was considerably changed in the final construction. George
> Grow, a son of Henry Grow, claims that this portion of the work was
> done without a comprehensive detailed plan, but was executed from a
> rough sketch drawn by Brigham Young and Henry Grow and from
> details which Mr. Grow drew as he went along. The lack of advance
> detailed planning is further illustrated by the fact that the design of the
> interior of the building was not started until April of 1867, a time at
> which the exterior of the building was demanding workmen qualified as
> finish carpenters. (A Tabernacle in the Desert, p. 98.)

Brigham Young's part in the creation was accepted by the
architect, who seems always to have felt the inspiration of the

man. Other architects involved with interior details recorded their respect as well. It also seems evident that President Young had respect for Grow's ideas. Both men were obviously excited and pleased with each construction development; this was not a labor of duty, but one of devotion.

The spirit of those who labored on the building is glimpsed in some of the newspaper accounts:

> Men . . . about the size of children's dolls are seen moving about on the top. We admire their nerve, but could not emulate it. . . .
> The lathers are hammering away with an earnestness that shows that soul is in the business. . . .
> We visited the place yesterday and were proud to see the men moving about with a heartiness that indicated a love of their work.
> When the President first spoke of the work, some anticipated that it could not be completed before the snow began to fall; but his energy and determination to do it seems to have been shared by the workmen and the job has been done in a marvelously short space of time.
> There are great faith and magnificent works operating in that building just now. (Ibid., pp. 40, 47-49.)

A chain reaction of spirit was evident from the leaders to the workmen and from the workmen to the building. The Tabernacle grew with increasing spirit as much as it grew with hammers.

A people who would make the first structure in an empty valley a place to hold church services was not to be stopped from holding conference in a building with only half a roof or an organ that had only fifteen feet of its forty-foot design completed. Joseph Ridges was able to make part of his organ perform in the conference of 1867; cloth was hung over the unfinished construction to make its appearance more presentable. As the organ sounded its voice in the vast space that could contain a six-story building, those who attended that conference must have sensed a spiritual feeling of greatness.

Brigham Young studied the great gulp of air the building was reaching out to grasp, and decided the space was still not enough for those who would yet come to worship. Provisions had already been built into the structure for the eventual construction of a gallery; the balcony was actually started in 1869. An unusual feature of the balcony design was its separation from the wall. About three feet of space was left open between balcony and wall for air and sound to move freely.

From the beginning Church leaders as well as members of the congregation had been concerned about the acoustical qualities of the building. The burst of inspiration to improve the acoustics with the unique gallery was rewarded. With intense interest President Young went to the Tabernacle when the gallery was finished to test the sound. The empty building responded warmly, but without a congregation he still awaited the first meeting with a hope that had roots clear back in the first Sunday in the valley.

After that first meeting, the May 21, 1870, *Deseret News* reported:

> While President Young was addressing the congregation, his hearers kept very still, and we are informed by persons who sat on the seats where they were accustomed to sit last summer, that yesterday they heard as they never did before. The gallery had made, judging by their experiences, a great improvement in the acoustical qualities of the building. The reverberation that was noticed on every previous occasion when a meeting was held there, did not exist yesterday. (Grow, pp. 88-89.)

Brigham Young was pleased; the first public structure erected in the untouched valley of 1847 had a most worthy descendant to fulfill one of his first dreams.

The Tabernacle has since become a popular tourist attraction; travelers from every continent have come to visit. Those who wish to test the building's acoustics are given the opportunity of hearing from a distance of nearly 200 feet the sound of a pin dropping. Many visitors come to listen to the Tabernacle's rich musical sound. Others come to weigh ideas. Some come to study the building's architecture. Those who come never forget the building. At first look, many do not think it a beautiful building, but as their sensitivity grows to appreciate its design strengths—as its spirit is fully felt—the Tabernacle does become beautiful.

Internationally known architect Frank Lloyd Wright was one of those who sat in the Tabernacle. Wright was never a diplomat; when questioned about Salt Lake's architecture, he quickly condemned the babel of buildings he saw during his visit. But Wright made a major exception: the Tabernacle. Speaking with conviction, he said that the Tabernacle was one of the world's great buildings, a fine example of functional design, or in Wright's words, "organic design."

"Organic design" is a down-to-foundation term declaring that every part of any design should have a working relationship with all other parts of the design. Wright coined the expression to stress that a building, a painting, an advertisement, or a living room should be as much of an organic whole as a human being.

There is no better example of organic design than the Lord's human creations. Vital organs have an interdependency: lungs squeeze oxygen into the blood stream, the heart pushes blood to all parts of the body, the nourished body uses arms and legs to search for food for the gastrointestinal organs to draw out the elements to keep the lungs functioning, and so forth through a fantastic interrelationship of physical, mental, psychological, and spiritual elements. Wright felt that architecture should reach for that unity in the traffic flow through the building, heating systems, light and air, structural strengths, functional needs, psychological and spiritual elements, as well as in purely aesthetic considerations. A building in this view does not need nonfunctional decoration any more than the heart does.

When organic design is produced in a building or other artwork a spirit is quickened beyond the physical elements. Design that stresses decoration first really has no heart.

Frank Lloyd Wright could see in the Tabernacle a superb example of organic design. The great building achieved an aesthetic whole with functional interrelationships unified with both human and architectural spirit. Marble could not build it; gold could not buy it; the railroads could not bring it.

The idea of the organic Tabernacle started in the mind of a man of vision. He was motivated for selfless reasons to build a fountainhead for spiritual influences where many could come to share. The Tabernacle from start to finish was built on functional ideas working together in an organic sense. A protective cover to bring a large congregation into an all-weather enclosure was Brigham's first major functional consideration. All ideas forming in his mind would be driven through the focus of this function.

The second key functional need was sound. Any construction design that would help this cause was more important to Church leaders than was any fancy exterior.

Another important functional design was the axis of the building. Functionally the first consideration of a site is its relationship to the sun. The heat of sixty-five hundred bodies packed together can be uncomfortable in itself without a hot sun pouring through a skylight or windows to the west. The only side of the Tabernacle that does not have any windows is the side facing the hot afternoon sun of the summer. If the Tabernacle were on a north-south axis, both the morning and afternoon sun could be a problem. For the climate of the Salt Lake Valley, the Tabernacle is perfectly oriented. The designers also oriented the Tabernacle to complement the relationship between the temple and the Tabernacle. The axis of the Tabernacle supports the temple.

Another important point of site selection is its relationship to traffic flow. The Tabernacle has almost a complete circle of entrances to ease pedestrian traffic in and out of the structure. The site did not ignore drainage patterns either, and floods have never threatened the Tabernacle.

Another organic function was the ventilation and lighting. This relationship began with the engineering decision for the roof buttresses. To let in light, air, and people, the roof at the buttress point was placed twenty feet above the ground. To hold an arch of this size the buttress was made nine feet long and placed under the roof. The Tabernacle windows are thus protected with a nine-foot overhang as a natural result. Architect Folsom reported that "Between the piers will be openings for doors and windows, which can be thrown open at pleasure, which will make it cool and pleasant in summer and warm and comfortable in the winter." (Grow, p. 33.)

Almost every interior detail was considered with a functional approach also. Take the floor for example: to aid the congregation's view and hearing, a slant was designed—the east end is sixteen feet higher than the west end. Sixteen feet is the height of a building one and a half stories tall, but the size of the Tabernacle and the design make the angle seem small.

The problems of cleaning and painting the ceiling through the years would interrupt any service held in the building if massive scaffolding had to be erected. But the architects simply provided holes in the ceiling through which cleaning platforms could be suspended.

Thousands of decisions had to be made to bring the design to this stage of development and yet there is not one statement I have yet found that involves a decision of surface decoration. Architectural literature today stresses that the exterior of the building should grow out of the interior's function. The Tabernacle was built with a rugged honesty that we would appreciate in any person. Each part of the building has a purpose and joins in an organic whole. It is a remarkable achievement.

As early as 1868 a New York publication written by G. W. Pine stated: "The builders of the Tabernacle were obliged to achieve their goal through ingenuity and adaptation. The result was a unique edifice embodying many ingenious techniques. . . . Its design has been applauded as one of the world's most perfect specimens of architecture." (*Beyond the West*, p. 247.)

In 1971 a National Civil Engineering Landmark plaque was presented to the Tabernacle by the American Society of Civil Engineers. Samuel S. Baxter made the presentation, declaring

27

that the society felt that it was important to bring national attention to projects such as the Tabernacle, "which bears the stamp of genius." (*Deseret News*, April 3, 1971.) (Photo 27.)

There is no question to me that the building *does* bear the stamp of genius. But I feel that there is one step higher than genius: the Tabernacle bears the stamp of spirit. More than stone and wood, trowel and dowel, more than architectural triumph in a frontier beyond the edge of manufactured resources, there was a spirit that drove the minds who designed it —an aesthetic spirit in its design, a community spirit that led the workmen who sacrificed for its construction, and a divine spirit woven through the whole fabric of its creation.

A carefully made design sings of spirit beyond physical materials, and of the designer's heart and sensitivity. To know history, and that our ancestors built well, strengthens us. A communication between spirits has been made. To know that they built with a mighty spirit and achieved a masterpiece lifts us, teaches us, and opens our minds to sensitive and spiritual meanings.

14
A Part of the Heart of Art

*We have explored a few ways of
discovering spirit through various aspects
of the home and community.
An important discovery path is through
the arts themselves. The arts are
unusually capable of stimulating
sensitive and spiritual growth. We use
art in functional needs of putting a roof
over our heads and shaping the spoon for
our mouths, but the heart of art is its
expressive qualities, which we can study
in painting and sculpture.*

With a box of children's crayons, a pad of paper, and an
idea in the search for music appreciation, I attended a
concert in San Francisco. Listening for color, I searched the

crayon box for colors to match the orchestra's musical mood.

Purple seemed to fit the oboe's mournful melody, and pouring out all the empathy I could feel in the music, I pushed and twisted the crayon across the paper to meet the sadness and my own body's response to the rhythm. Small twisted lines, some thick, some thin, grew as the music grew. When the rhythm swelled, I would sway physically with the sounds, and my crayon echoed the sway in longer sweeps.

A trio of trumpets punctured the oboe's contemplations. Grabbing a yellow crayon, I tried to bring in the crisp action with sharp diagonal lines. My hand was always moving with the music as though I were part conductor, part dancer, and part musician. When the strings swept a nuance of tone that pulled together all of the instruments, the side of the crayon was used. A solo seemed to need the point of the crayon.

The allegro movement produced several of these abstract musical sketches. I snatched colors quickly to keep pace with the mounting tempo. The perspiration gathering on my forehead dropped a spot on the paper just as the cymbals crashed. Pleased with the coincidence, I quickly surrounded the spot with a yellow-orange undulating circle.

As the music pulsed to a climax, I was so involved in my graphic interpretations that I did not even notice that an arc of heads had formed around me from the row behind. As the last note trailed away with my crayon, I became aware of someone's breath at my ear. Turning around, I saw the circle of heads that had evidently been watching my drawings. The closest breath by my head began to become words; it was hesitant at first, then a gush of words that swish-whispered: "I always hated modern art; I detested it, I had believed that any modern artist must be a communist, or someone trying to destroy our society. When I watched your drawing coming out of the music, for the first time in my whole life I discovered that colors and lines are really music; they are beautiful by themselves. I could see music in the lines and I began to hear colors. Would you be willing to sell one of your sketches?"

I was so pleased that someone had caught a glimmer of vision that I made her a gift of them. She tucked the drawings into her program with such tenderness that I could tell how deeply it had moved her to see as well as hear music. I also realized that I had not been a passive listener; I had been an active participant in the music even though I had sat in the audience. Involvement had lifted my level of awareness and increased my appreciation too; I had enjoyed the concert more than any other person in the audience whose musical background might have been similar to mine.

Involvement is one of the quickest ways of discovering the spiritual dimensions of art. Artists often enlarge on their own experiences to bring spirit to their creations.

One evening while I was visiting in the studio of a young sculptor, Dennis Smith, one of his children came in. The artist broke his conversation with me and effortlessly moved into the world of children to empathize with the child's all-consuming self-concern. As I watched him, it was no surprise to me that his little sculptures of children were so sensitive. The artist and his child used words to communicate, but it was the invisible thread of spirit that linked them. Dennis was the greater energy, and as he empathized with the child I could actually witness his energy moving into the child's being. With the child's purity of spirit he could cradle the father's energy, but Dennis was nourished in return. When his spirit was pulled to sculptural purposes, the power of that force made dynamic design.

Dennis has filled his sketchbooks with children at the business of being children—at their games, in their thoughts, with mother, in lanky adolescence, with the bloom of infancy. Years of drawing children, of studying their nature and inner spirit, of writing poetry about them, of playing with them, of working with them, and of crying with them have resulted in two marvelous things about Dennis: the children have made him more sensitive, and he has captured the expression and the spirit of children in sculpture.

Children at their games show tremendous imagination. Imagination cannot flower without spirit. A child's imagination can place him in the pilot's seat of a pencil. Zooooom—the pencil moves in an arm-stretching arc through space. The childish fingers that hold the pencil in its supersonic flight are not visible to the fearless pilot. The rubber eraser flames with full throttle and the freshly sharpened needle nose leaps for the clouds. The pilot takes a quick look over the yellow side of his aircraft to see the earth dropping away to marble size. With a twist of the fingers the plane banks and roars into a steep dive for the clouds far below. Stomach muscles tense as the pilot pulls back on the stick just in time to prevent a crash. Another sharp bank and the plane sideslips across the sky. Waving to the admiring crowds on earth the pilot calls over the roar of his engines, "Hello, Grandma!"

Who can find a father who still owns a pencil pilot's license? Dad's imagination has been grounded. As fathers we often fail to realize exactly how important play is to children. I have come to know that an airplane my friend and I built in the empty lot back of my childhood home was an important signpost on my way to imaginative spirit. That involvement, in recollection, helps me to understand children and some of the subtle threads of art.

Our airplane was big enough to sit in. Our parents saw it as a massive pile of junk; we saw it with our imaginations as a mechanical marvel. I spent hours in the flying machine, twisting knobs from an old alarm clock, taking an altitude reading from a broken thermometer. I remember the exciting moment when I came in over the landing strip of the empty lot. I could see the anxious faces of my father and mother below as they came running with the news that I was landing with only one wheel. My engine was also sputtering and through the choking sounds I could hear the fire engines racing to their positions. It would take steel nerves and veteran experience at the stick to make it with a dangling wheel. I moved the plumber's friend gently and felt the wings respond. Then with a swoop I made a perfect one-point landing. As I climbed out of the cockpit my mother rushed up and said she knew I could do it. I pushed back my flying goggles; I knew I could, too.

Mother called me into lunch about then and I think I swaggered up to the back door. While I ate my sandwiches my attention was still on the wonderful flying machine I could see in the empty lot. The wings wired to the friendly trees hadn't been scratched in the landing.

Not until this writing had I stopped to think about the contribution the empty lot between our house and Otterstrom's had made to my boyhood. That empty lot and flying machine lifted my youth to the stars. My favorite book became *We* by Charles Lindbergh. He had flown the Atlantic and I could almost see *Us* in the title of his book. It was more than play, it was a spirit that made flights to the impossible, an excitement of growing in our capacities, a reach for the joys of life.

28

When I met Dennis, I met a man who knew all these things about childhood and adolescence. In the clearest terms he touches my own memories of youth; he captures the mystery and joy of all youth. To walk among his works and sense their spirit is to peel years off our ages. Every time I see one of his exhibits I feel that I know a bit more of what life is all about. His work should be "required seeing" for students in teacher education or for prospective parents. He parts the way in my search for sensitivity and spirit.

The child in the rocking chair (photo 28) is coming in for a landing with his airplane dangling one wheel. Life is hanging by the same wire that holds the flapping wheel; the ground is rushing up, but this child, alert in every stroke of clay, has the confidence that his imagination can guide him. He could also be seeing himself as a bird about to leap into the air for his first flight from a perch, or just a boy enjoying the kinesthetic pleasure of movement itself. The sportsman stepping from his sleek racing machine has felt no more thrill of movement.

Perhaps the boy is testing the rocker—for children delight in suspense. How far can he lean before the ultimate tip? The floor is only a hand's reach away, but the spirit the child feels brings him to the edge of the Grand Canyon.

This is not a sculpture of a boy; it is a sculpture of a boy's spirit.

The artist increased the statue's energy by making the shirt with individual pieces of beeswax. If he had smoothed the shirt into a freshly pressed and starched one, spirit would have been ironed out.

Sympathetically the back of the chair bends to the forces that seem almost tied to the back of the boy. The chair's back and the boy's converge rather than parallel each other. When lines converge, a dynamic quality is created. Another diagonal line swings from the youth's head down through his legs. This swing is echoed by the rockers of the chair, which are so necessary to balance not only the boy's weight, but also the forces he exerts. Force opposing force makes drama. I lean forward myself to witness the suspense of forces probing each other with the boy's balance held on edge.

If the child's imagination can make a chair a flying machine, imagine a flying machine made *for* imagining! (Photos 29, 30, 31.)

Smith has created an art form that is unique; in the spirit of a child's vast imagination, he has fashioned flying machines

29

and other marvels from clocks and cogs, springs and things, and all that a child's treasure hunt for visual delights could discover. With welding torch instead of his sketching pencil he joins rods and wheels to the energy of his imaginative machinery. When a Dennis Smith bronze boy steps aboard, not even an empty lot next to the Otterstroms is necessary to make it zoom into the clouds. Nothing on earth can hold it down. Nothing seems impossible. It is as though a fresh breeze were to blow through us.

These sculptures are the freshness of uncontaminated youth —a child running to be picked up by a loved father, a little girl talking to her doll, a boy helping a widow with her groceries— these fragments of freshness calm our anxieties. They are more than the sentimentality of lesser sculpture. To be involved in a Dennis Smith sculpture or machine is to wipe out worries for a moment.

So often people with limited imagination will say, "I don't know anything about art, but I know what I like," and what they like is usually a *surface* enjoyment of what they view.

30

31

Dennis has a way of peeling off the surface for us to see the more vital inner spirit of children. He does this with such skill that any viewer willing to pause can see below the surface of an artwork for an understanding of his own childhood and the children that come into his family harbors.

Examine the picture of the Dennis Smith creation of a child in a submarine of his imagination. (Photo 32.) Knobs and gadgets are the spirit guiders of the underseas voyage. The boy is

the master of the machine, which in turn is the master of the mysterious sea. The awesome forces of the sea quickly capture a child; a boy viewer who loses himself in his study of this artwork may find himself mastering a new confidence and lubricating his own imaginative awareness.

Children find water irresistible; they are unable to resist playing with the garden hose, carefully stepping in each puddle on the way home from school, or stirring a small stream with a stick. Growing up does not change the fascination. On a college canyon picnic, many students sat by a mountain stream and stared for twenty minutes at the rhythmic, dashing patterns. The cook's call, echoing down the canyon to "come and get it," did not stir the water watchers. They were hypnotized by the liquid movement. When young people let a call for food slide past, there must be strong forces at work enriching their sensitivities.

Without such things as canyon streams or Smith's sculptures we could forget the enrichments we once learned. The search for sensitivity and spirit is often a search to recapture what we once enjoyed. Dennis Smith helps me to remember and recover, and then lifts me to new exploration. His imaginative submarines stir again my fascination with water and the magnet of machines that pulled me as a boy. Then, as I discover the artist's aesthetic sensitivity in forming these creations, I begin to form new insights on my own frontiers that lift my sensitivities to discover higher spiritual things.

In contrast with the freedom of imagination in the submarine sculpture, observe the sculpture of the young girl. (Photo 33.) She is between two worlds; she hesitates, feeling, as do many children, the questions of a child's life in an adult world and the insecurity of the space between the two worlds.

This sculpture of a child's spirit searching for anchor is thoughtfully sensitive. It has a beautiful simplicity. The liveliness of childish action is restrained, but still not stiffly dead in her frozen apprehension. A string stretched from the center

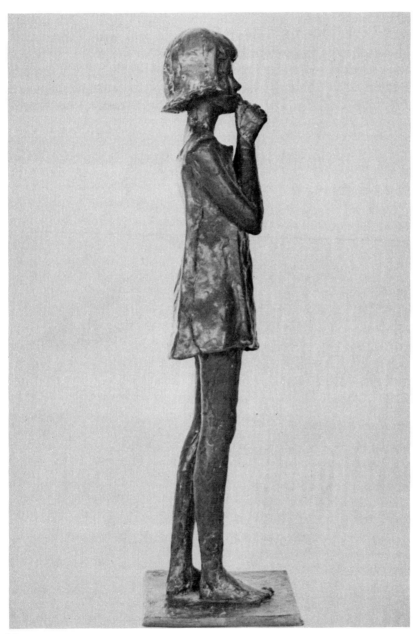

33

of her neck to the right ankle immediately reveals the differences in shapes of the front half and the back half of the figure.
These differences, which deny stiffness with simple rhythmic
lines, assure us that the heart is still beating, though the breath
may be held. There is a quiet but effective balance of shapes in
this held breath. The Hogarthian line through the simple

34

shapes of the legs carries a soft, lyric movement. Small details such as the hem of the skirt projecting more at the back than at the front provide a better design plan than dividing the space into monotonous equal parts. The axis of the dress and head take the same direction, while the neck, hands, and leg harmonize in parallel lines with a different direction. The dress has not the starched precision of a mind resolved; the drapery lines help tell the hesitancy. She could be a child approaching her probing mother who holds an empty cookie jar, but that interpretation would be less significant than the concept of a child approaching adolescence.

Spirit speaks more warmly in the sculpture of a mother and child. (Photo 34.) The mother has a strong, secure position integrated with the chair, while the child bends her back with more animation than the previous figure. With economy of strokes, Smith gives the child a question in her face which the mother seems to answer with the conclusion, "and we will always love you."

Two more sculptures from the chair series are the figures of a young boy sitting on a stool and an older girl on a chair. (Photos 35, 36.) The boy sits with a "What's next?" attitude, but not worrying about the consequences. The girl expresses more sophistication in her spirits, as though she knows the boy is but a child and that he too will have to live through childhood. But she still looks to the adolescent future herself with some concern, and the security of the chair of "now" is more sure. Sophistication and concern give more spine to her moment of contemplation, while the boy is completely at ease. The boy's figure is sculpted with a looseness that fits the ease of one who can seldom find a comb, while the girl is more precise, like a young lady caring for long hair and reluctant to wear the same dress two days in a row. Details such as these point out differences in the spirit of a boy who lives for the day and a girl thinking of the future.

Our search for sensitivity does not end in the discovery of these details. As we remember our own search for reality as adolescents, do we see the youth of our day more sensitively?

One final example: Most of us as parents have been aware of the affectionate bonds that children form with dolls. Some children have more love than one doll can hold, and a parade of dolls lined up on the couch is necessary to prevent a bursting. When only essentials could be tucked into pioneer wagons rolling west in the wilderness, few wagons with children did not reserve space for a doll. A student of children, as is Dennis Smith, could not overlook this theme.

Look at the sculpture of the child with a doll in her arms. (Photo 37.) The box and legs have an angularity that is often associated with children and young adolescents, but the tilt of the head and the look of the child have the blooming spirit of motherhood. In this photograph no features of the face are seen except the slight silhouette, but it is less a head to be studied in its various parts than a flow of spirit from the head to the cradled love.

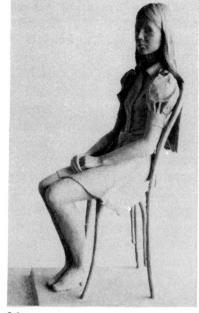

35   36

37

Spirit is communicated in what artists call gesture. The angularity of the box and the child's legs does not carry into the head. Angularity creates a contrast that strengthens the curvilinear qualities. The rounding forms help create a lyric mood and the doll's head reflects the outpouring of a lullaby of knowledge. A walk with a friend of trees, even one who has love and spirit. Now there is a challenge—to create a soft lullaby in resistant bronze!

When a child leaves a doll, the life it enjoyed in the play-mother's hands suddenly dies. The doll lives only with the spirit of the child. Dennis Smith's sculptures of children live warmly in the hands of a sensitive appreciator, but when the sculpture is placed on a table by itself, it does not die. Dennis has sculpted into his bronzes a permanent spirit to treasure— that of the inner lives of children.

15
Seeing with Aesthetic Vision

*Our own childhood explorations and
our experiences with children can lead us
to sensitive discoveries about ourselves
that prompt an appreciation of life.
Then, with growing sensitivities, we can
achieve artistic expression.
If we turn directly to the work of
significant artists, we can discover many
sensitivities to lift our senses of appreciation and to magnify the spiritual
essence.*

One of the most tragic figures in art was Vincent Van
Gogh. Probably no artist was ever as lonely, and no human
being probably ever wanted to share so much. No one cared for

his pictures. No one cared if he lived or died except his brother, Theo. Theo cared so much that after Vincent died, he suddenly died, too. It is appropriate that they are buried together in the little cemetery at Auvers, France.

On one of my visits to the graves I found in the ivy in back of Vincent's tombstone a palette left by a German artist. In a moving spirit the artist had carefully printed *Fur Vincent* in the center of his palette, the wellspring of his own paintings. He then had left it as a gift.

Van Gogh has devotees today in all corners of the world. Those standing reverently at his grave speak many languages. To look at their faces is to see thoughtful people all thinking in the same language of spirit about a man they have come to respect, though never seen. Van Gogh did not change; his pictures did not change. Those who ignored the man in his day and those who stand respectfully by the grave today differ only in their perceptions and sensitivity; those willing to reach have found Van Gogh's spirit in his life and in his work. Here is a testament of the existence and greatness of spirit, and of the high importance of education in opening our eyes. The eyes Van Gogh met in his life were mostly closed.

The deep, almost terrible longings of Van Gogh might never have been known if Theo had been like everyone else. Vincent poured his feelings into letters to his brother that give us a personal, inside view of an artist in a unique way. With the artist's stomach crying for food, and only enough francs in his pocket to buy either a tube of paint or a bagette of bread, Van Gogh returned to his easel rather than to the table.

He painted himself so deeply into his pictures that once when someone asked if his painting were a picture of a sunflower he seriously reported, "That is not a *picture* of a sunflower; that *is* a sunflower!" He followed his brush in so deep that he felt he was painting the flaming sun itself.

One of Vincent's letters to Theo told of his trials in painting some beech trees. Hours went by and he was not satisfied. He wrote of the great strength of the soil, and that he could not

SEEING WITH AESTHETIC VISION   165

get the roots to reach down into the firm ground for nourish-
ment. At the height of his struggle to capture the dynamic
forces at work he snatched a paint tube and squeezed paint
directly onto the canvas as roots. Churning with new insights,
he modeled the roots with his brush.

As he stepped back to observe the results, his shoulders and
whole being must have relaxed. The tree had grabbed the
earth, had taken root, and would live. To make a tree live is to
paint its spirit.

A rewarding experience for a person who has not had much
experience in art but is anxious to learn is to take a tree-trip. A
beginning point for such a trip is at a good art museum. If
museums are not available, obtain a good art book from the
library. Search out pictures of trees and take time to study carefully the trunks of the trees. Do not look to see how well the
artist has applied his paint; that different criterion is still
important, but this is a spiritual search. What kinds of spirit
does the tree speak? Does it thirst, reach, dance? Does it seem to
reach out with a sensitive affinity for other trees? Does it have a
personality? Does it have substance that is more than a veneer
cosmetic job—sincerity, not a tricky flashiness? After an
earnest examination of pictures in a fine museum, go to a sidewalk sale where pictures are sold for twenty dollars. Make the
same examination.

Those who take serious tree-trips should come to see that
the trees in mediocre paintings are like cardboard fakes, pasted
on the canvas as stage props rather than rooted into the
ground. Trees without spirit will seem hollow as though they
were painted on cardboard and wrapped around nothingness.
Study trees long enough and you will become excited about tree
personalities.

If trees at this point are for you still little more than fence
posts, the search for sensitivity should be even more of an
acknowledged necessity. Dedication has a way of opening eyes.
Seek out a friend who knows much about trees and ask for a
tree-walk. People who love trees will be pleased to share their

knowledge. A walk with a friend of trees, even one who has never touched a paintbrush, will delight willing eyes. Then return to an art museum and discover how much more your eyes will see in a landscape painting by a fine artist.

Try me if you are low on tree friends. One summer I borrowed some trees to study near a friend's cabin in the mountains. Join me in the broad hammock stretched between two tall trees and let me show you what I saw then. The fir tree at the foot of the hammock seemed pleased that someone would stop to look. (Photo 38.) The shaft of the trunk shot in a straight line for the sky like a rocket, and because of its sparse branches at the bottom I could see almost its full height. I was delighted by the aged, needleless lower branches; the toothless twigs created new linear patterns. For the first time I noticed that many of the branches curved out from the trunk. I have always painted pine trees with the main line of the branch stabbed into the trunk like a spear, but these branches and twigs moved in a lyric swing that delighted the squirrels that frolicked their aerial pathways.

38

These little animals, incidentally, are great ones for a tree-walk. They helped me see the relationships of the branches with each other as they skipped along from branch to branch with never a dead-end twig. Artists often talk of "continuity of line," and as I watched the squirrels and chipmunks play tag I saw as never before how the twigs do relate to each other in beautiful patterns. I looked again and the tag game had become a ballet. The branches were not broomsticks; they swayed with the symphony of rhythm.

A rider on a horse clopped into the canyon and the little squirrel tails went swishing after their owners into the nearest underground tunnel. I frowned at the loss but quickly relaxed as the rhythm of the horse's hoofs became a syncopation that I found myself humming. I began to notice new rhythms in the branches. All of the branches were orchestrating. Even the dead branches still sang of their former aliveness. The little twigs bristling at every angle with offshoots had an electric energy about them that caught the syncopation.

As the music faded I began to see the spaces formed between the branches and twigs, a mosaic of lights. Each space was different from its neighbor and yet all of them curled toward a harmony of expression that found resemblances in this family tree. The openings shifted with a slight breeze and suddenly I saw a natural stained-glass window of sky blue. Can you see it with me? Beautiful rhythmic patterns—and organ music drifted into my mind. Organ pipe trunks of trees pushed up their dignified lines to the windows for a calm reverent feeling. The neighboring evergreens repeated the organ and cathedral lines. The hillside beyond was alive with a movement the ears could not hear—visual movement for the eyes. It is easy to take a tree-walk with your eyes and not even move your feet. It is easy to enjoy sensitive things if we but look. Looking with others makes it easier.

Five hundred years ago Michelangelo was creating a statue of Moses. The first time I saw his Moses, the statue was so alive with energy that I could feel the chips of stone bursting from the sculptor's hammer and chisel almost as though I were there when he carved it. Ever since then I have longed for the impossible dream of a trip back through time to sit in his studio and watch the Moses statue being created. If you enjoyed the tree-walk, try a time-walk and sit with me in Michelangelo's studio.

There would be no timid taps of the chisel, but rather a shower of marble dust rising from blows driven from the depths of the artist's being. The statue itself tells of this heat of creation, as well as inspiration. Michelangelo's face would be so intense that I would not dare risk a question, for it would mirror his sculpture of a prophet who has just returned from a direct communication with the Lord only to find his people already straying from the truth. The carved eyes of Moses turn to the people and stare in incredible disbelief. Every nerve and muscle of the statue leaps into agitation over the wide chasm between ignorance and revealed truth. (Photo 39.)

Michelangelo understood the concept of revelation as much as any man of his times. The great artist believed that he was divinely called to be a sculptor and that the Lord illuminated his mind. The Moses statue helps me to appreciate Michelangelo's awareness of this principle. Every element of the sculpture breathes the confidence of a spiritually guided Moses. Michelangelo intended it to be so. The sculptor raised stone horns on the head of Moses; to me they symbolize the rays that connect God and man, symbols of spirit, for Moses has just received the commandments from God. Michelangelo translated even the beard of the prophet into a generator of spiritual energy. There are no languid forms anywhere: the drapery churns into the climactic moment. The left foot slips back, the toes tighten to push the huge figure out of the chair. We would likely push back our own chairs not to be in the way. As we watch Moses burst from the rock we quickly learn that the statue is not a pile of static stone, but a spiritual force.

Now come with me and visit a modern painter. Franz Kline's early artistic explorations were forays of futility. He

39

returned each time empty-canvassed. His friend, DeKooning, watched this labor and finally asked what it was that he was seeking.

"For clarity, for the statement that can be read only one way."

Then one night Kline sat staring at the white shield of blank canvas in almost a frantic frustration. His biographer says that he first thought of a woman, a real, warm woman "merged with all the clap trap of dead symbolism of the academicians; she was a Leda, pinky, voluptuous, entwined with the swan in all the antique foliage. And there on the palette were heaped all the sumptuous colors of Boucher and Titian ready for another tinsel allegory—symbols, symbols—and then THE symbol had loomed—stark, black on the white canvas. A dozen sure swift slashes and the painting was done." (Blesh, *Modern Art U.S.A.*, pp. 273-74.)

Those of you who have enjoyed the beauty of Oriental characters may find a ready echo, but basically Kline's picture is one of raw, intense, slashing spirit.

Some of us have made such slashes across the front of a term paper when the writing was not going well and our frustrations were triggered. (Photo 40.) The explosive strokes probably relieved a bit of tension, but at the same time the strokes were likely very expressive lines with logarithmic curves that would be difficult to duplicate elsewhere as beautifully. That these strokes were made with spirit cannot be questioned. That they were made with meanings beyond the lines themselves is also self-evident. Every stroke released energy, and the catharsis made frustration that ignited the explosion less disturbing. Explosive scribbles should have more aesthetic significance than a carefully painted flower that is precisely detailed but has ramrod stems and shoehorn petals. Stiff, detailed, brittle flowers in rigor mortis have no spirit.

There is no plea here that you fall in love with the paintings of modern artists. One can have favorites among many artists. My hope is that you will find a sensitive link with the spiritual life of paintings and sculpture. Whether the art is enjoyed or not, it should be acknowledged that artists such as Kline or Jackson Pollock painted with an expressive spirit that poured out of their brushes.

Jackson Pollock died at a young age in a violent automobile

40

crash, but in his short life he created an art idea that exploded across the American and European art centers. The names of his imitators would fill a phone book.

For some years before his famous innovation, Pollock had been working on paintings of twisted faces, she-wolves, and other fragments of dreams at night. Then came his painting that was almost a picture of a collision itself. Staring at his former work he felt the nothingness of spirit, and with a lip-biting decision he threw his canvas on the floor, dodging the smash of the falling easel. Perhaps it was then that he threw some paint on the floor-sprawled canvas. As he stared at the slithers of paint on the wounded white surface, something in his own spirit felt a sympathetic reach. It ignited a fuse, and leaping to his feet he grabbed buckets of paint and the collision was on. Blesh says that he began to throw paint across the canvas, "racing around it with pails, hurling gashes of violent hues to splash and flow, to glut and to congeal, clots and rivulets, freshets of excitement, layer after layer of blot and blob and of weaving, tangled lines. Hours went by until the pails were empty and the fury over. Pollock squatted on his heels in a corner, trembling and spent, looking out over the exaltant, screaming chaos that lay on the floor. Jackson Pollock was looking at a totally new way of painting. Almost all night Pollock sat looking at that picture, and slowly before his eyes it changed; order marshalled itself in all that wilderness. Those violent forces—the whirls, the plunges, the thrusts began to float in an equilibrium of violence against violence. It was a miracle, a miracle like the atom loaded galaxies orbiting themselves." (Blesh, *Modern Art U.S.A.*, pp. 254-55.)

Perhaps it might help if I suggest the analogy of an orchestra conductor. He is less likely to obtain a sensitive response from his musicians if he stands as stiff as a sword swallower and waves his arm like a mechanical rock-cracker. To pull the full musical mood a fine conductor uses his whole body, animated with his spirit, to feel the music and to inspire his orchestra. His movements are like those of an expressive dancer.

With this image in mind, picture Jackson Pollock caught up in a deeply personal expression where his body moved to the rhythms of his creation—to the extent that the paint was less dumped on the canvas than strewn as a visual pattern in the wake of his rhythmical movements. That is, the paint was a visual trailing of a choreography. (Photo 41.) The seemingly haphazard patterns of Pollock's painting were in a very real sense a picture of the inner spirit he had felt during its creation.

Rembrandt van Rijn has become known as one of the greatest artists of any century. Of special interest to our search, he has been recognized as a "spiritual man in an unspiritual age." In that day, portraits that looked like bodies stuffed with straw, and group portraits of people all lined up like a row of bowling pins, were being painted by many Amsterdam artists. They were portraits of monotony covered with monotony as far as young Rembrandt was concerned. As he viewed these group portraits of solemn faces staring out of the flat canvas at nothing and held together only by the frame, he resolved at age

41

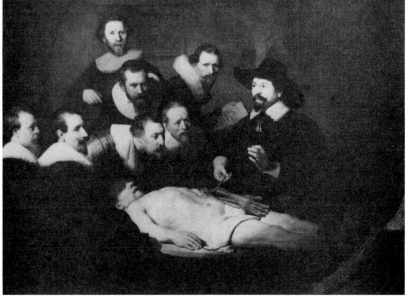

42

twenty-six that his new commission to paint six doctors would have more spirit.

Rather than simply picturing six men standing independently in a row holding their degrees, Rembrandt searched for a common spirit that held these men together. Their natural interest was medicine, so he selected the incident of Professor Tulp giving a lecture on the anatomy of the arm. All the portraits tie to this moment. (Photo 42.) Every face has an individual spirit; each man is reacting to the lecture in an individual way. I hope Rembrandt won't mind if I pretend some exaggerations to illustrate. The man in the center could be saying, "Oh no! That last operation I did, I must have connected the wrong parts!" The man to the lower left, "What deftness, what skill! Professor Tulp is a remarkable surgeon." Over his shoulder looks a man who might be saying, "It's a brilliant lecture but I could surely show them a thing or two." In the upper left corner the response seems to be, "I've heard this lecture twice before and I even know where the jokes come in." The man at high center might say, "Good night, I think I left the toaster on." Actually, he holds a list with the names of the doctors.

The most important part of the head is the eye. Look at the eyes of each man and compare them with the others. Rembrandt used the eyes as a major expressive tool in building his portrayal of each man's spirit. I have become so fascinated with the range of expression that I have photographed or acquired over forty slides of close-up views of eyes Rembrandt painted. Every time I show them to students I continue to be amazed at the vast expressive spirit and characterization he painted into eyes.

Place any Dutch painting made in 1632 alongside the Tulp painting and the difference between the heads done by Rembrandt and those of his peers is enough to demonstrate that his search for human spirit was successful. While others labored to paint eyes, noses, and mouths, and often painted them well, the paintings are exactly that: pictures of faces with eyes, noses, and mouths. Rembrandt was searching past these features into the heart of the person to reveal his character. His brushes painted features not as anatomy but as clues to the personality of their owner. His greatest paintings were yet to come, but he already was a painter of spirit.

Rembrandt has often been called "The Master of Chiaroscuro." *Obscure* means to darken; *chiaroscuro* means light and dark. In the Tulp group the chiaroscuro has not come to its full measure, but it should be easily apparent that there is a lively light and dark pattern. The Master of Chiaroscuro used his light wizardry more with biblical subjects. Rembrandt was a student of the Bible through his beloved mother's influence, and his lifetime work drew heavily from these themes, especially in the tragic later years.

Especially significant to me is that in materialistic Holland, Rembrandt made not one but several paintings and etchings of the Emmaus chapter in the testament of the Christ. He started one of the paintings, "Supper at Emmaus," (photo 43) near his twenty-second year. Jesus was placed in complete silhouette in front of the strongest light. The brightest light radiates from the profile of the Christ into the room with a nuance that gradually darkens until the far ends of the house are shrouded in black. The floor and table's legs are lost in the dark. Facing Jesus across the table is a man. Most viewers of the painting would not start their examination of the picture by analyzing how well the nose and eyes were painted; instead, the viewer immediately feels the astonishment of the host as he becomes aware that the Son of God is sitting at his table. The host's total spirit is captured as Christ is revealed: it is that of the passerby who has not recognized who He is—in Christ's time, in Rembrandt's time, or our time. Perhaps we are something like the woman in the background, going about our affairs without awareness. No detail is given of the woman's face or costume; she is revealed only by a small spotlight.

Jesus forms a diagonal line of movement that is repeated by the perspective line on the wall and the angle of the woman's

43

back. The host dynamically slants in the opposite direction, and this slant is repeated by the woman's arms and a small shadow behind Jesus.

Conversation at the table is not whether the toast was burned or buttered. Rather, the dramatic light persuades instant belief that this is an unusual moment of import. That the dead can live again is more than an editorial page statement. Rembrandt's.own feelings are brought into focus, not the flighty wishes of a pompous sitter for a portrait. Rembrandt makes a declaration that the spirit overcomes physical mortality—a declaration more beautiful and powerful than any petty paragraph of words. Painters facing their easels for a lifetime of painting details of objects, the likeness in portraits, the surface of material, have missed what Rembrandt had mastered at college age.

If all of Rembrandt's self-portraits could be gathered into

one gallery there would be stunning evidence of three conclusions: the role of spirit in art, Rembrandt's role as an "old
master," and an autobiography of a man that is as telling as it
can be made. A study of Rembrandt's painting of his own face
is one of the most interesting experiences one can engage in at
an art museum. The Louvre usually has only two of his self-
portraits on exhibit, but these two alone show the inner forces
of a life and reveal in intimate detail how his inner spiritual
forces changed through the years.

No portraits I have ever seen touch my feelings more than
Rembrandt's. In his earliest self-portraits I see a young man
brimming with confidence and enthusiasm, even arrogant in
his confidence, sure of himself, sure of the world. Those eyes are
not as teachable as the later ones, but they are clearly readable.
Then his self-portraits become more serious as he struggles to
find the meanings of life and his work. I can sense him suddenly
realizing that he does not have all the answers, that life is a
design as much as his paintings.

No blow battered him so much as the illness and death of
his beloved wife, Saskia. She left a void that he could not face
and his anguish echoed endlessly in the chasm. That anguish
pours out of his eyes in the self-portraits of these years. The
paintings are not of a man openly crying at the tomb, but an
introspective turmoil of a man wrestling with his emotions.
More than just paint and canvas, there is an intensity of spirit
that cannot help but be a moving experience for anyone who
will pause to look into the eyes of one who has given his full
confidence, who hides nothing, but looks for trust and understanding—expecting none.

After Saskia had been lowered into the grave under the
small organ of the church, no one could find Rembrandt. On a
hunch, one friend went to the studio to find him still in his
funeral clothes, black gloves and all, working feverishly at his
easel. Rembrandt in his concentration did not hear the man
enter; he did not feel the touch on his shoulder. He was painting a picture of Saskia—he was reaching for her spirit.

Part VI
The Search for Spiritual and Sensitive Powers

16

Spiritual Energy

As a human being is much more than
bone and muscle, so is a building more
than timber and dowel, or a painting
more than oil and canvas, or a statue
more than clay and armature — it is spirit
that gives life and meaning.
But life and meaning can vary in degree.
Spirit may lightly nudge a gesture or it
may be a powerful source of energy. The
pursuit of spiritual leverage and the
storage of spiritual energy should be
essential parts of the search.

Electricity is an invisible energy. Drawn from a reservoir such as a battery or a hydroelectric plant or a nuclear furnace, it becomes power. Attached to something of a certain design, this power becomes useful to man. If we were to turn off all switches to these reservoirs, the machines of medical miracles would stop, automobiles would not ignite gasoline, appliances would be worthless, and light bulbs would only remind us of how much we have depended on this invisible power. We would lose more than comfort; our world population has grown so vast that we could not now sustain ourselves without electricity to run our food production machinery.

Spirit is a greater invisible energy than is electricity. Drawn from a reservoir within the arts or from a human being or from a divine source, spirit becomes power. Attached to something of a certain design, spiritual power becomes useful, if not essential, to man. If we were to turn off all spiritual switches to these reservoirs, we would not have the drive to harness electrical energy, to solve energy problems, to split the atom, or to walk on the moon against mind-stretching odds. To turn off the power of spirit would be to remove all that is good and beautiful in the world and to reduce man to a barbarian. It is in the realm of spirit that two people fall in love, that a slightly built mother holds back the rolling weight of an automobile as her baby crawls from danger near the wheels, or that a hero makes a sacrifice in war. From a theological position there would be no world at all if there were not spiritual power.

Skeptics of the invisible essence of art or religion seem to accept rather readily in our day the physical miracles of science. In yesteryear it was not so—they laughed at Fulton, Galvani, and others who could see the invisible power of steam and electricity. I believe that Fulton and Galvani were drawing understanding from an inner personal reservoir of a spiritual nature; the skeptics with horse-and-buggy minds were without personal reservoirs to contain ideas of higher energy.

At the three-quarter point in the twentieth century our world faces an energy crisis. Men of vision see one of the greatest potentials for energy in the hydrogen of water. The problem that specialists in physics face is to construct a container to hold this nuclear energy—to form a reservoir.

When the hydrogen container is eventually achieved it will not be a tank of steel, glass, or concrete; these materials are too puny to withstand the tremendous heat generated by a hydrogen furnace. The research of some scientists exploring this potent power is directed toward the creation of a container formed from electricity—an electrical field encircling the energy —an invisible energy containing a higher energy, not the static stuff of steel. The physical world creates miracles difficult to understand.

Spiritual energy is also volatile and cannot be contained without a special kind of reservoir. The container of spirit is not a box, a battery, or a book. To make definitive statements about spiritual energy and how it is stored within a human being or a work of art is difficult—more truly, it is impossible.

The container of spirit is not glass or steel, nor do I think it is bone or tissue. The strong feelings we sometimes have seem to burst from within us at times as though a reservoir had burst and we were suddenly flooded with a warm comfort. The idea that spirit bursts out of nothing is untenable. My hypothesis is that spirit is held in a reservoir that is made of other spirit of a lesser energy. I believe spirit can be pulled together to form a stronger reservoir for a higher spirit. This means to me that the sensitivities one discovers and enjoys with small things can generate the spirit for an aesthetic reservoir, which can in turn build a stronger reservoir for divine forces.

I believe spiritual reservoirs begin with the first step on a search for sensitivity. Each sensitive discovery sparks a spiritual charge that circles the nucleus beginning. The orbit increases with additional spiritual discoveries: a new sensitive awareness of color, a deeper meaning to a line of scripture, a mighty change in the heart.

Because this spiritual reservoir is not static steel, but energy itself, it must be continually charged or it will shrink as quickly as it can expand. Linked sensitive and spiritual experiences are essential. Charles Darwin in his advanced years lamented that he had lost his taste for fine music. His sensitivities to the music that he had loved so much in his youth atrophied because of his failure to let aesthetic things be nourished. He had poured all of his energies into science. I couldn't understand as a youth how a high churchman could crash from spiritual heights to excommunication; I know now that an energy reservoir needs care and nurturing.

There are things that we can do that will help to create spiritual reservoirs, to enlarge them, to discover the spiritual potential of others as well as ourselves. In creating reservoir space we must first be aware of our potential and realize that we have not come anywhere near to tapping our personal capacities. We may be looking at ourselves as people looked at the patent office a generation or two ago: they believed that the patent office could be closed soon, because they thought all the possible inventions had been discovered.

When the value of acquiring a more alert set of senses is recognized, there is still the next step of having the desire to probe actively into the stirrings we feel, to multiply them into a more clear-cut part of our personalities. When we have the desire to enrich the spiritual aspects of our lives, all of living becomes a more joyous thing. If living is not a happy thing for us we may have concentrated on too few facets of life without an awareness of other key needs, and we may have missed acquiring the desire to be sensitive.

The third step is to form a serious plan for achievement. Whatever our age, nature has something to teach us. Leonardo da Vinci said his greatest teacher was the eye. He found an unusual sensitivity as he studied nature, watched the birds, and made a design for a flying machine more than three hundred years before the Wrights flew their aircraft. A program of seeing, reading, and meditating are important paths in the search. To set foot on these paths, with a resolve to make each day a step inward, may be to find eventually John Milton's "Apostrophe to Light":

> . . . Shine inward, and the mind through all
> her powers

Irradiate; there plant eyes; all mist from thence
Purge and disperse, that I may see and tell
Of things invisible to mortal sight.

17
Exploring Sensitive Thought

*The search for sensitivity in aesthetics
has intrigued thinkers for centuries. We
should not miss their light although their
divergent conclusions need the gospel's
guiding directions.
Thought itself is an important spring-
board in the search for sensitivity.*

There is design in thinking. The meaning a person finds in
the universe and in his position in the universe helps him
understand life; it gives his life actions, beliefs, and values. It
helps him develop concepts of good and evil; it gives him a
definition of terms. Truth, reason, and beauty are surely
auspicious beginnings to any individual's thinking.

Philosophy, a kind of thinking that seeks wisdom and
understanding, cannot be a substitute for religion or art, but it

does ask questions related to a search for sensitivity and spirit. It begins with a division of human experiences into six major areas of thought:

1. Logic—What are the methods of exact reasoning?

2. Epistemology—What is truth and what are the limits of validity?

3. Ethics—What is good (the ideal character) or moral?

4. Aesthetics—What is beautiful?

5. Metaphysics—What is the essential nature of reality or spirit beyond the reach of the senses?

6. Axiology—What are values or value judgments?

In man's struggle to answer these six questions, he developed four different theories or schools of thought. The oldest of the four, *idealism*, relates the most to the spiritual dimensions of art.

The Greek philosopher Socrates felt that the greatest virtue was knowledge. In the Socratic view it was not enough to say, for instance, "I like art," or "Man should live a moral life." Socrates thought it was important to know what is *meant* by aesthetics, or to know the *meaning* of morality. He pushed each student to "know thy self," for he believed that all persons had within themselves whole thoughts, if they could be sensitive enough to discover them. In this view, each of us has an existing creative and aesthetic nature to be discovered or enriched. Since the answers are already within us, Socrates believed that merely to listen to a lecture was not enough; he felt sensitivity was best achieved through questioning.

Aristotle, a follower of Socrates' illustrious student Plato, believed that all persons are capable of art expression as well as of enjoying art experiences. To deny these qualities is to limit our thinking. We must nurture all of our abilities if we expect them to function for us.

I believe that each of us has a divine spirit that emerges in the same way—in direct relation to the nurturing we give it. If we agree with Socrates that answers are within our beings, then any form of nonphysical growth—that is, any development we reach for that has spirit roots or good roots—will help free or increase that divine spirit.

Some theologians see aesthetics, or the study of the beautiful, as being in opposition to divine growth. I see no grounds for faith-damaging conflict between religion and aesthetics. Indeed, there is an affinity here to augment, not destroy. There are two kinds of art, just as there are two kinds of religion—one good, the other, spurious.

The arts, as much as any subject, can lift civilization or lead to its decline. Religion can lift civilization with a Christian caring for underdeveloped nations, or it can be the battle zone for a senseless civil war. The artworks of a falling empire become increasingly inferior; the spirit of a falling religion becomes increasingly weak. The arts can build or destroy spirit in like manner.

We cannot dismiss the keys to an aesthetic life on a personal whim without probing for understanding of the whole idea. Aesthetic spirit and religious spirit should not be divorced; they should constitute a wedding where two kinds of spirit augment each other.

Consistent with such augmentation, the Greeks said, "Man is the measure of all things." Aristotle's teacher, Plato, looked at man as the measure of all things, but he looked for what man should become, not what he is. Michelangelo shared that goal. He painted Adam on the ceiling of the Sistine Chapel as the ideal man, as one of the sons of God, not a man one could see on an Italian street.

Ideas, Plato stressed, were more important, more real, than actual objects. That is a great idea in itself. We usually think that what we can touch is real—a rock, a face, a clump of earth. If we accept Plato's idealism, then we must agree that what a child draws is much more significant as an idea than as a realistic representation. An artist's expressive purpose, his ideas, must be an early, important consideration in measuring the value of his art.

Does this suggest that a painting's meaning is more important than its existence? Maybe the meaning *is* the existence. If we were to meet the Savior, we likely would be more interested in his existence than in what his existence means. We bring the meanings. It is the viewer who is in judgment—not the Christ, not the painting. The painting obviously exists, as does the Savior. We will have an aesthetic or spiritual experience, depending upon what we have built within us. If we have faith in the Savior's existence, he can draw the meanings out of us. In the same way, a good painting can pull more from us than can a weak picture.

In Descartes's search for an absolute, or at least a basic reality, he arrived at his famous declaration: *Cogito, ergo sum*—"I think, therefore I am." If we *think*, then we have proof that we exist. If we *feel spirit*, or know spiritual things, then we have self-evident proof that spirit exists.

The idealist elevates man out of the animal world and holds that men and women are unique creations of God, capable of responding to spiritual stimuli not experienced by animals. This spirit is more important than any physical law. No Olympic contestant became a champion without believing that he could be a champion. Idealism stirs a person's mental machinery to confidence; spirit provides more energy for the muscles; and the goal provides direction.

The idealist believes that beauty already exists. If it exists, and it is good, the desire for growth urges its examination. If refining of the mind, the idea, and the spirit become primary goals for us to reach, I firmly believe that the refining of our senses has a key role in our comprehension of those goals and in the logic of our achieving them. This refining has an important role in elevating the quality of aesthetics, as well as in polishing the lenses that will help us probe beyond our present experiences.

Several philosophers share this belief. An examination of some of their ideas lends a sensitive insight to art's spirit.

Immanuel Kant (1724–1804)

As philosophers probe for the forerunners to Kant's ideas,

they find that much of what he believed was by no means original. He had read extensively and had incorporated much of what others had previously said into his own framework. This was perhaps his greatest achievement: to be able to reconcile differing opinions and seemingly contradictory notions into one consistent, systematic whole.

When Kant approached aesthetics, he was not interested in offering judgments about the qualities of particular artworks—though he did refer to specifics to illustrate his arguments—but he was instead interested in establishing what the role of judgment itself is. He was trying to explain what judgments entail, what their prerequisites are, when we can and cannot fairly judge, and what it is about certain objects, such as artworks, that makes them subject to aesthetic (as opposed to moral or scientific) judgments.

Kant said that true art should be "without purpose." We could reformulate the expression to read, "A work of art should not have any other purpose than to be an aesthetic expression—that is, an artwork is not a tool nor does it have economic worth as part of its aesthetic value, nor can our personal taste in any way influence the merit of the work." When we are looking at a painting in the proper aesthetic manner, questions about the cost or where it was purchased or who painted it are totally irrelevant. Similarly, if we use the painting as a door-stop or merely as something to cover up a crack in the wall or harmonize with a rug, we are giving it some kind of purpose instead of treating it as an artwork. Kant made the plea that we treat a painting as what it should be: a painting! If we search for sensitivity, we need to seek intrinsic worth. All of this is akin to looking at a flower because it is beautiful, regardless of whether it can be eaten or used for fertilizer.

This is what is meant when we say that a painting of Jesus is not necessarily better than a painting of Satan, that our inclination to favor the Christ is not an aesthetic judgment. To analyze this statement we must recognize that when we say that we would rather have a painting of Jesus hanging in our home, we are in fact not talking about the painting at all. Certainly a cartoon figure of the Christ cannot compare with a Rembrandt drawing of Judas Iscariot—when the artwork of the latter is treated in the proper way.

The challenge that Kant gives us is to learn to search out what is good in something. This challenge should emphasize for children's development many opportunities for exploration into artworks of excellence. One of the great errors we make in decorating our homes is that we hang pictures that are aesthetically weak, that have a surface prettiness, an empty spirit. A veneer painting without spirit carries the risk of teaching children to identify themselves with mediocrity. It has been stressed that spirit gives the spark to a person's life; an artwork is flabby without this essence. We must not let children, or ourselves, accept flabby work as an ideal.

Many of us cannot afford to purchase paintings for our homes of the quality found in the best art galleries, but many of the important galleries' best pictures were purchased inexpensively before the artists were accepted. The sensitive eyes of the first purchaser saw aesthetic values, while others, not as sensitive, missed these qualities or were even stupid enough to ridicule them. We may never attain a curator's skill, but we can search and learn about the factors that these perceptive critics discovered, and we can enjoy exploration in books and museums for other facets of aesthetic merit and spirit.

Art lovers with modest budgets may do well to visit a university student art show. Usually the art faculty will sit as a jury and numerous weak works will have been screened out. Those accepted for the show have already met several aesthetic tests. The chief designer for the Church magazines uses his aesthetic skills to acquire student works along with mature works from various exhibits. His home is an adventure to visit—artistic surprises are at every corner. Children in this home are receiving a powerful education in aesthetics, in sensitivity, in appreciation, and in life itself every time they walk through his garden, sit in excitingly designed rooms, or enjoy his extensive collection of artworks: paintings hung on walls, sculpture standing at visually arresting points, outdoor art in the garden, and stacks of prints made available in convenient racks for browsing.

Children do "catch" taste from their environments. One California teacher with a very sensitive outlook loved to collect interestingly shaped bottles. The varieties of shapes and the distinctiveness of each bottle was a continuing visual delight to the young teacher. When I visited her classroom I noted these bottles sitting on a shelf, arranged to appeal to the eye. She never made any comments about the bottles to her students, but one day a small boy came running in breathlessly to show her a beautiful bottle he had found by the side of the road as he walked to school. He gallantly presented the bottle to her, and she accepted the treasure with an inner pleasure, for the child had discovered and shared a new awareness of beauty with her. Who had told him about beautiful bottles? The bottles themselves in part, but he would likely never have seen the bottle on the side of the road any more than did the thoughtless person who had discarded it as litter, if it had not been for a teacher who cared about bottles and loved them herself. The student had caught the spirit of the teacher's love of common things, things she had come to learn were beautifully shaped.

Friedrich Schiller (1759–1805)

While Kant argued that the moral value of the subject matter of a painting had nothing to do with its qualities as a painting, Schiller made an important distinction. Schiller, while wholeheartedly accepting the Kantian separation, said that the pursuit of quality in paintings has in itself good moral ramifications. Schiller believed that if a man pursued an understanding of art and learned what separated the good art from the bad, this very process would have a beneficial effect on his life. In a home where the child hears good music, regularly sees flowers beautifully arranged on a table, and is taught how to read the great classics in literature, that child will more likely have a balanced, even temperament, and will probably treat people more sensitively. Schiller adds that if the child learns to find the qualities that make artworks great, he will be more capable of recognizing what qualities he would want within himself.

Benedetto Croce (1866–1952)

One word often associated with Croce is *expression*. He looked upon art as a form (or maybe *the* form) of expression. When an artist creates a masterpiece, he is saying, "This is how I feel about such and such." He is not just stating a casual position, as might an impartial sports writer or a person who is writing a pamphlet on how to assemble a Comfy Collapsible Chair. The artist is letting us know his opinions, his fears, his feelings, his hatreds, his loves, his ideas—his very spirit. The artwork is an expression of the artist; it is filled with comments about his life and his attitudes towards the world.

As observers or spectators of art, our challenge is to uncover what it is that is being expressed. This is not done by reading a biography about the artist or even statements that the artist might make about the artwork.

Children so often produce work that easily slips within the folds of the great thinker's thoughts; they attack an expressive problem directly and sincerely, giving clear-cut expression of their fears, feelings, hatreds, loves, and ideas. We need to be able to observe art just that directly and sincerely to see what has been uttered and what the various nuances might mean. In seeking to uncover the subtleties between the sincere and the insincere in art, our ability to discern the same in people (and introspectively within ourselves as well) is a valuable capacity for any one of us to have. In learning what is trite and insincere in art, we learn to understand what it is in ourselves and others that makes our daily expressions honest, thoughtful, and rewarding.

Martin Heidegger (1889–1976)

Heidegger, a very influential philosopher, attempted to show how the viewer, not the artist, comes to grasp or to understand what the artwork reveals. He is concerned that we have a meaningful relationship with the artwork, that we let it reveal its many ramifications to us. One of the great tragedies of modern man is his making of the beauties of the world into mere *things*. When the price of paper and wood products rises, trees seem to lose their value as things for just looking at, or for having a picnic under, or for joyfully climbing. We convert our meaningful experiences into economic goods.

Our challenge as human beings is to allow ourselves to be open, to be receptive to the phenomena of the world. We are not supposed to merely submit objects to rigorous scrutiny in an attempt to find what *use* they might have for us, but are instead challenged to open ourselves and see what the things in themselves are. Heidegger gives an example of what we should look for in a particular painting, "The Peasant's Boots," by Vincent Van Gogh:

> From the dark opening of the worn insides of the shoes the toilsome tread of the worker stands forth. In the stiffly solid heaviness of the shoes there is the accumulated tenacity of her slow trudge through the far spreading and over uniform furrows of the field, swept by a raw wind. On the leather there lies the dampness and saturation of the soil. Under the soles there slides the loneliness of the field-path as the evening declines. In the shoes there vibrates the silent call of the earth, its quiet gift of the ripening corn and its enigmatic self-refusal in the fallow desolation of the wintry field. This equipment is pervaded by un-complaining anxiety about the certainty of bread, the wordless joy of having once more withstood want, the trembling before the advent of birth and shivering at the surrounding menace of death. This equip-ment belongs to the earth and it is protected in the world of the peasant woman. From out of this protected belonging the equipment itself rises to its resting-in-self. (Hofstadter and Kuhns, *Philosophies of Art and Beauty*, p. 663.)

When we observe any artwork we should allow it to say as much as is possible. We need to look carefully and sensitively. But there is more in a painting of shoes than an affinity with the wearer and the fields. When we explore the design and feel

it sensitively, we will begin to see why the art masters are truly
masters and why the "artists" who make tricky illustrations
seldom convey very much. Spirit cannot survive on little
mediocrities; an art spirit, or any spirit, must have deep roots.

18

Stretching Sensitivity's Stride

*In summary, spirit is the essence of every
significant human activity. To become
more sensitive to this key essence in its
various forms, and to link these forms
for cumulative strength, must be the
greatest search in each life.*

*The primary cornerstones of the future
are the family, the community, and the
church. Today's most critical problems
declare a need for more cohesiveness
in these areas—and cohesiveness thrives
on the linking of spiritual elements.*

*One of the best fields for a rich spiritual
growth is in the arts. We make our
temples, our homes, or our lives no more
beautiful or perfect than we have gained*

the sensitivity to make them beautiful.
We fail our stewardships if we do not
follow the admonition of President
Spencer W. Kimball to lengthen our
strides in providing a wide spiritual
atmosphere in all facets of life.

If spirit stops, all is dead; eternity cannot be.

A kingdom can fall, but a people of animated spirit will rise again. A forest can burn, but roots dug in deep can grow again. A man can die, but his spirit can live forever. The eternal life of spirit should not be more of a mystery than is mortal birth.

But even as the miracle of birth is not without labor, spiritual achievement is not without labor. The labor of lengthening a stride almost automatically produces spirit.

Bondage that binds the spirit of man reduces his stride to a shuffle without the effort of resistance. Bondage that binds individuality reduces man to a robot. Bondage that binds the spirit of a painting produces the mediocrity of a paint-by-number work.

When President Kimball urged church members to lengthen their stride he knew that the spirituality of the membership would be intensified. Christ urged the man in bondage to go the second mile, to double his stride. The second mile is a gift of spiritual independence that removes the veil of insensitivity to a destiny.

When I walked with Helen Keller at Bushnell, I felt the energy of a remarkable spirit at my side and I watched her perform a miracle with that spirit to make the men of Bushnell live again. Her great labor to see without eyes, to hear without ears, burst the shell of insensitivity that bound her and she was shaken free to generate a greater spirit, which penetrated every man in that hospital room. I was convinced that spirit can be created.

When Sadhu burdened his chances for survival and walked against fate, his life was snatched from the storm and preserved. The strength of our spiritual convictions can measure mortal and eternal lives.

When I walked with Tommy at the turkey ranch, we were not thinking of the eternities. Small walks can start big strides, and on that day the sensitive outlooks of both boy and father were stretched. There are many small walks in the journey to sight that can, in combination, make a difference to all eternity. Too many years passed by before I fully realized the great strength of small sensitivities; a major reason for my writing these pages is the hope that younger parents might catch what I missed in spiritual vision.

The search for sensitivity and spirit need not be a lonely walk. We can walk vicariously with Rembrandt and Van Gogh in the art galleries and they can teach much of life as well as art. The great always have long strides, and we must push our spiritual and aesthetic muscles to keep pace. If we are sensitive enough when we walk with the spirits of the great, their energy can be transferred to us.

We can walk with sensitive people through the pages of history. We can reach back as we read the ideas of dedicated men and women. We can walk in spirit through the scriptures with the prophets.

We can learn much from the living in our search for sensitivity and spirit. My daughter had polio many years ago. Those who know her story have walked by her side as she has manipulated her braces and crutches. They all tell me her spiritual stride is difficult to match and that there is a distinct inner quickening awakened by being in her presence.

Each of us has at some time walked with someone who pulled us into lengthening our stride. The exhilaration of spirit we felt then is waiting for release in every corner of our environment if we will but search and renew our spiritual reservoirs.

When we walk with a man of science and we are sensitive enough to lengthen our perceptions, we can more quickly appreciate the accomplishments of the mind. When we walk with an artist and we are stretching our sensitivities, we can more quickly appreciate the accomplishments of the heart. When we walk with the Christ and we lengthen our spiritual stride, we can more quickly appreciate the accomplishments of the soul.

The wholeness of our spiritual philosophy is usually best influenced by those with whom we have walked—by whatever philosophy has grown up in us, the material or spiritual, and whatever experiences we have personally or vicariously stored in the chambers of our beings, the sensitive, aesthetic, or religious. All these influences will make our decisions for tomorrow, for the future, for the eternities. Any of us can look to the past and wish certain decisions had been better made. If only we had stretched our stride more with those who gave us room at their sides, if only we had enriched our lives with more meaningful experiences, if only we had been more sensitive in understanding our opportunities, we could have avoided hurts of many kinds.

Tomorrow we face new decisions—will it be with sensitivity's stretched stride?

Art has helped me to see and understand the spiritual things of God. From my drawing I have been awed at the magnificent expressions of design, especially human design. The world and its population were not created by accident but by design—an aesthetic, sensitive, divine design. Artistic people who have not found the divine spirit declare themselves when they abuse the sacred in art. I have come to know that a true spirit of art can live comfortably in the soul, and if our children do not learn the wholesome attributes of art they may plunge to negative forces in art's domain that are as strong as any forces they will ever combat. A search for sensitivity and spirit will let us come to know that aesthetic and spiritual forces can together lift us to the highest exaltation of man.

An artistic creation signals an artistic eternity. It is inconceivable to me that a universe of such intricate design could fall apart in the eternal future. There are many skills we leave behind at death; aesthetic appreciation obviously makes a bridge.

If we expect to participate in the eternal design, it seems self-evident that we must lengthen our aesthetic and spiritual strides. We do this through hard work, selfless service, listening to whisperings of the spirit, purity of heart, tuning ourselves to hear subtle things, sharpening our focus to see delicate design, and placing Christ in the center of that design. In any corner of our world the spirit is there; we need only to walk to meet it, we need only the sensitivity to see it.

Paul was one who walked to meet spirit. He began as a weak man, but his stride rose to catch the spirit, and he left one of the most important messages about it:

> And I, brethren, when I came to you, came not with excellency of speech or of wisdom. . . . And I was with you in weakness, and in fear, and in much trembling. And my speech and my preaching was not with enticing words of man's wisdom, but in demonstration of the Spirit and of power: . . . Eye hath not seen, nor ear heard, neither have entered into the heart of man, the things which God hath prepared for them that love him. But God hath revealed them unto us by his Spirit: for the Spirit searcheth all things, yea, the deep things of God. For what man knoweth the things of a man, save the spirit of man which is in him? even so the things of God knoweth no man, but the Spirit of God. Now we have received, not the spirit of the world, but the spirit which is of God; that we might know the things that are freely given to us of God. Which things also we speak, not in the words which man's wisdom teacheth, but which the Holy Ghost teacheth; comparing spiritual things with spiritual. But the natural man receiveth not the things of the Spirit of God: for they are foolishness unto him: neither can he know them, because they are spiritually discerned. (1 Corinthians 2:1-14.)

Spirit searches all things, and we will not know anything in a sensitive way without it. Art can be foolishness to those without spirit. Artists who lack spirit in harmony with the gospel can destroy. Good art is a schoolmaster in spiritual discernment.

A wide-eyed girl with tears trickling down her face so startled me in an art museum I almost collided head-on with a sculptural masterpiece. Recognizing her as a member of my travel group, and fearing someone had stolen her purse with the all-important passport, tickets, and money inside, I rushed to her side and anxiously inquired about her tears.

She simply pointed to a statue in front of her and said, "It is *so* beautiful!"

The unexpected answer left no words in me to reply. I breathed a sigh of relief and left her, but her comment echoed back and forth in my mind and I could not look away. I turned my full attention to the girl, who was still deeply entranced with the statue. There was a glowing freshness about her, and I began to notice that other gallery visitors were becoming more attracted to her than they were to the statue. I could see a spirit of aliveness about her that the other visitors did not seem to have. Looking back at the statue I knew there was something below the stone's silent facade that was broadcasting to this girl, and she was receiving with full power. The more I studied her the more I wished I were standing in her shoes.

Most of my life has been spent in artistic pursuits, but I have never *cried* in front of an artwork. What elements in my life had stopped me from having such a full experience as that which had given that young student her brightness? What had stopped me from having tears? What had stopped the other gallery visitors from having tears? What had we missed?

About then another gallery visitor walked by and hardly gave the statue a thin glance. My self-criticism eased a bit; I had at least found some aesthetic pleasure and enjoyment in studying the artwork.

Three of us, three viewers of the same sculpture: one found a flood of beauty brimming in tears, and another dropped a brief glance that plopped in the pool of his experience without a ripple. What I saw was invisible to the glancer; what my student saw was invisible to me.

Natural man or spiritual man, natural art or spiritual art—

we receive that which we have gained the sensitivity to see. The student's tears in front of a statue were sensitive tears formed from discoveries in appreciation of the beautiful. Her life was a spiritual life formed from a sensitive appreciation of spiritually walking with her Father in heaven. Sensitive strengths gained in one spiritual dimension can boost sensitivity in another spiritual dimension. A family enjoying an aesthetic experience together multiplies rather than merely adding to family ties. To walk with music can quicken the step. To see with art opens other visual doors. To walk with my student, or even the least of the spiritual affinities, is to walk with Him from whom all spirit of beauty flows.

Postscript

The worth of a man does not consist in the truth he possesses or thinks he possesses, but in the pains he has taken to attain that truth. For his powers are extended not through possession but through the search for truth. In this alone his ever growing perfection consists. Possession makes him lazy, indolent, and proud. (Lessing, Gesammelte Werke, vol. 13, p. 23.

In the world's beginning, Lucifer's plan that all would be saved was rejected. Man was not to be denied his free agency. Some have come to believe that one needs only to acknowledge the Christ to achieve salvation, but salvation was not intended to be so painless or growthless. Even Christ did not escape pain. Growth comes more surely with sweat, struggle, and pain.

To possess a single truth cannot be enough for eternity. Progression is an eternal principle, and one of the greatest eternal sins must be to deny this progression. Anyone who says, "I am saved," and stops his search, loses his salvation at that very point. Anyone who achieves a great testimony of the gospel with even much effort and then stops his search for more truth becomes Lessing's victim of pride and indolence. We were placed on this earth to become searchers, eternally to grow.

My conviction that *spirit* is the most important word in the English language, that spirit is limitless and that it embodies every aspect of life from His Holy Spirit down to the kind of spirit we place into a menial task, leads me to believe that spirit must be a major goal for life's search. I believe not only that a search for sensitivity and spirit will never end, but that the very act of searching is a form of spirit. I also believe that the aesthetic part of spirit stirs essential generators within our beings that produce eternal growth. These generators power our senses and activate the mechanisms of true happiness.

Aesthetic sensitivity is not an end in itself. But if we look around through the eyes of a Neutra we can see much unnecessary ugliness in our homes, churches, communities, and other elements of our environment; it is evident that no matter how much truth we possess, even divine truth, we must remain aesthetic searchers. "If there is anything virtuous, lovely, or of good report or praiseworthy, we seek after these things." (Article of Faith 13.) To seek or search, with a lengthened stride, for spirit and sensitivity could be the greatest step in our lives.

Bibliography

Anderson, Donald M. *Elements of Design*. New York: Holt, Rinehart and Winston, 1961.

Arnheim, R. *Art and Visual Perception*. Berkeley: University of California Press, 1954.

Bates, Kenneth F. *Basic Design: Principles and Practice*. Cleveland and New York: The World Publishing Company, 1960.

Beitler, Ethel Jane, and Lockhart, Bill C. *Design For You*. New York: John Wiley and Sons, 1961.

Binyon, Laurence. *The Spirit of Man in Asian Art*. Cambridge: Harvard, 1935.

Blake, Peter. *God's Own Junkyard*. New York: Holt, Rinehart and Winston, 1964.

Blesh, Rudi. *Modern Art U.S.A.* New York: Alfred A. Knopf, 1956.

Bowness, Alan. *Modern European Art*. London: Harcourt Brace Jovanovich, 1972.

Bruton, Michael J. *The Spirit and Purpose of Planning*. London: Hutchinson, 1974.

Burton, William H., and Heffernan, Helen. *Creativity: The Step Beyond*. Washington, D. C.: National Education Association, 1964.

Canaday, John. *Mainstreams of Modern Art*. New York: Holt, Rinehart and Winston, 1959.

Covey, Stephen R. *Spiritual Roots of Human Relationships*. Salt Lake City: Deseret Book, 1970.

Cowley, Matthias F. *Wilford Woodruff: History of His Life and Labors as Recorded in His Daily Journals*. Salt Lake City: The Deseret News, 1909.

de la Croix and Tansey. *Gardner's Art Through the Ages*, 7th ed. New York: Harcourt, Brace and World, 1975.

Dorfles, Gillo. *Kitsch: The World of Bad Taste.* New York: Universe Books, 1969.

Faulkner, Ray, and Ziegfeld, Edwin. *Art Today: An Introduction to the Visual Arts,* 5th ed. New York: Holt, Rinehart and Winston, 1963.

From Sea to Shining Sea: A Report on the American Environment— Our Natural Heritage. Washington, D.C.: The President's Council on Recreation and Natural Beauty, 1968.

Gill, Eric. *Beauty Looks After Herself.* New York: Books for Libraries Press, 1966.

Gombrich, E. H. *The Story of Art.* New York: Phaidon, 1951.

Graves, Maitland E. *The Art of Color and Design.* New York: McGraw Hill, 1951.

Grow, Stewart. *A Tabernacle in the Desert.* Salt Lake City: Deseret Book, 1958.

Hart, Frederick. *ART.* Vol. I. Englewood Cliffs: Prentice Hall, 1976.

Henri, Robert. *The Art Spirit.* Philadelphia: Lippincott Co., 1951.

Herberholz, Donald and Barbara. *A Child's Pursuit of Art: 110 Motivations for Drawing, Painting, and Modeling.* Dubuque: Wm. C. Brown Co., Publishers, 1967.

Hesiodus. *Theogony.* New York: Oxford, 1966.

Hofstadter, Albert, and Kuhns, Richard. *Philosophies of Art and Beauty: Selected Readings in Aesthetics from Plato to Heidegger.* New York: The Modern Library, 1964.

Janson, H. W. *History of Art,* 3rd ed. Englewood Cliffs: Prentice Hall, 1969.

Leeuw, Gerardus. *Sacred and Profane Beauty.* New York: Holt, Rinehart and Winston, 1963.

Lewis, C. S. *Christian Reflections.* Grand Rapids: William B. Eerdmans Pub. Co., 1967.

Lindbergh, Anne M. *Gift From the Sea.* New York: Pantheon, 1955.

Linderman, Earl W., and Herberhoiz, Donald W. *Developing Artistic and Perceptual Awareness: Art Practice in the Elementary Classroom,* 3rd ed. Dubuque: Wm. C. Brown Co., Publishers, 1974.

Linderman, Earl W. *Invitation to Vision: Ideas and Imaginations for Art.* Dubuque, Iowa: Wm. C. Brown Co., Publishers, 1967.

Lowenfeld, Viktor. *Creative and Mental Growth,* 3rd ed. New York: Macmillan Publishing Co., 1957.

Lowenfeld, Viktor, and Brittain, W. Lambert. *Creative and Mental Growth,* 6th ed. New York: Macmillan Publishing Co., 1975.

Martin, Betty. *Miracle at Carville.* New York: Doubleday, 1950.

Mendelowitz, Daniel M. *Children Are Artists.* Stanford: Stanford University Press, 1953.

Myers, Bernard. *McGraw-Hill Dictionary of Art.*Vol.4.New York: McGraw Hill, 1969.

Neutra, Richard. *Survival Through Design.* New York: Oxford University Press, 1954.

Newton, Sir Isaac. *Principles, Book III: The System of the World, General Scholium.*

Osborn, Alexander F. *Applied Imagination.* New York: Charles Scribner's Sons, 1957.

Parnes, Sidney J., and Harding, Harold F. editors. *A Source Book for Creative Thinking.* New York: Charles Scribner's Sons, 1962.

Peckham, Morse. *Man's Rage for Chaos.* Philadelphia: Chilton Books, 1965.

Pine, C. W. *Beyond the West.* Utica: Griffiths, 1868.

Pyper, George. *Romance of an Old Playhouse.* Salt Lake City: Seagull Press, 1928.

Reisman, David; Glazer, Nathan; and Denney, Ruel. *The Lonely Crowd*. New Haven: Yale University Press, 1950.

Rogers, L. R. *Sculpture: The Appreciation of the Arts/2*. London: Oxford University Press, 1969.

Rubin, William S. *Dada, Surrealism, and Their Heritage*. New York: The Museum of Modern Art. Distributed by N. Y. Graphic Society Ltd . Greenwich, Connecticut, 1968.

Sakanishi, Shio. *The Spirit of the Brush*. London: J. Murray, 1939.

Snygg, Donald, and Combs, Arthur W. *Individual Behavior*. New York: Harper Bros. Co., 1949.

Taralon, Jean. *Lascaux*. Paris: Caisse Nationale des Monuments Historiques, 1960.

Thomas, W. I. *Primitive Behavior, an Introduction to the Social Sciences*. New York: McGraw Hill, 1937.

Tibbitts, Clark, compiler. *Aging in the Modern World*. Ann Arbor: University of Michigan, 1957.

Tunnard, Christopher. *The City of Man*, 2nd ed. New York: Charles Scribner's Sons, 1970.

Untermeyer, Louis. *Modern American Poetry*. New York: Harcourt Brace and Co., 1942.

Wahlquist, John T. *The Philosophy of American Education*. New York: The Ronald Press Co., 1942.

Wyman, Jenifer D. *Primer of Perception*. New York: Reinhold, 1967.

Periodicals

Beck, J. "Babies Love to Learn." *Parent's Magazine*, September 1967, pp. 58-59.

Branch, Gilman and Weber. "Monitoring Community Noise." *Institute of Planners Journal* 40: 266-67.

Greenberg. "Accelerating Visual Complexity Levels in the Human Infant." *Child Development* 42:905-18.

Hunter, Howard W. "The Tabernacle." *Ensign*, November 1975, pp. 94-96.

Kessen. "Visual Response of Human Newborn to Linear Contour." *Journal of Experimental Child Psychology* 13: 9-20.

Korner, A. F., and Grobstein, R. "Visual Alertness as Related to Soothing Inneonates: Implications for Maternal Stimulation and Early Deprivation." *Child Development* 37:867-76.

Leroi-Gourhan, Andre. "The Evolution of Paleolithic Art." *Scientific American*, February 1969.

Maughan, Walter L. "Paul's Thing." *Instructor*, May 1970, pp. 155-57.

Neutra, Richard. "The Mormons and the American Community." *Improvement Era*, February 1960, pp. 82-83, 112-13.

Rebelsky and Hanks. "Father's Verbal Interaction with Infants in the First Three Months of Life." *Child Development* 42:63-68.

Walters, C. P., and Walk, R. D. "Visual Placing by Human Infants." *Journal of Experimental Child Psychology* 18:34-40.

Zimmerman, Carle. *Time*, December 28, 1970.

Index

Acoustical qualities of Salt Lake
Tabernacle, 141
Aesthetic sensitivity: developing, 47,
63; lack of, 92-94. *See also* Sensitivity
Aesthetics, 187-88
Airplane, imaginary, 149-50, 152-53
Anatomy lecture, painting of, 174
Anchor as Christian symbol, 105
Apathy, risks of, xii, 26, 88
"Apostrophe to Light," by John
Milton, 184-85
Architecture: evolution of, 52-53; for
children, 70-71; incompatibility of,
with spirit of occupants, 77-78;
functional requirements of, 121;
effect of, on spirituality, 124-25;
Salt Lake Tabernacle as great
example of, 134-45
Aristotle, 187
Art: definition of, 23; good and evil,
28; reveals a group's spirituality,
28; first principle of, is unity, 49;
capacity of, to stimulate spiritual
growth, 146; surface enjoyment of,
153; modern, 168-72; effect of, on
civilization, 188; for its own sake,

190; arrangement of, in designer's
home, 191-92; connection of, with
morality, 192-93; as expression,
193; sacred nature of, 199
Artists: lack of appreciation for, xii,
163-64; popular, are not necessarily
good, 119; significant, studying
works of, 163; modern, 168-72;
walking vicariously with, 198-99
Artworks: of children, 8-14, 193;
labeling mediocre objects as, 56,
191; Church-related, 95, 120-21;
of quality, seeking out, 191
Ataturk, statues of, 94
Axiology, 187

Beams, hand-hewn, 57
Beauty: children can appreciate, 28-29,
63; bringing, to homes and yards,
62; natural, 95; idealists' view of,
189; converting, into economic
goods, 194
Beliefs, connection of, with design, 129
Bell tower on Berkley campus, 123-24
Bicentennial year, beautification programs of, 62

211

Blake, Peter, 96
Bodies, organic design of, 142
Bomb shelter, neighbors join in
    building, 85-86
Bondage: visual, 89-90; spiritual, 197
Boots, Van Gogh's painting of, 194
Bottles, collection of, 192
Boweries built by pioneers, 135-36
Brigham Young University, professor
    desiring position at, 79-80
Buildings, spirit of, 134. See also
    Architecture; Church Buildings
Bushnell General Military Hospital,
    4-6

Car repaired by Dutch family, 45-46
Cathedrals, 130
Chance, achievements come not by,
    xiii
Chapel: transition to spirit in, 118;
    Parisian, members refrain from
    visiting in, 126-27
Chiaroscuro, 175
Children: artworks of, 8-14, 193; can
    appreciate beauty, 28-29; making
    objects interesting to, 47; growth of,
    factors contributing to, 48-49;
    artistic stimulation of, 63;
    architecture for, 70-71; handling,
    in church, 125-26; empathy for,
    148; imagination of, 149-50;
    sculptures of, 151-62
Christianity, symbols of, 104-6
Church buildings: design of, 77,
    124-25; symbolism of, 110; clutter
    in, 116
Church of Jesus Christ of Latter-day
    Saints, artworks of, 95, 120-21
Civic design, 97
College students, weakness of faith
    of, 25
Columns of spirit, 26-27

Committee for designing foyer decor,
    120
Community spirit, 79, 98; of various
    cities, 80-81; as related to function,
    82
Corter, C.M., 48-49
Crayons taken to concert, 146-48
Creativity, loss of, 15
Croce, Benedetto, 193
Cross, symbolism of, 104-5

Dance classes, 15-16
Darwin, Charles, 183-84
Decisions, facing, with sensitivity, 199
Decoration: rule of thumb of, 56;
    integrating, into total design, 61;
    in foyer of Church buildings,
    116-19
Descartes, 189
Design: poor, 50-58; of homes, 59-61;
    civic, 97; potential distractions in,
    115; connection of, to man's beliefs,
    129; evidence of, in creation, 199
Dolls, children's bonds with, 160
Drawing at symphony concert, 146-48
Dutch family, help offered by, 45-46

Egyptian architecture, evolution of,
    52-53
Energy: spirit involves, 40, 181-83;
    electrical, 181-82; reservoirs for,
    182-84
Entablature, 53
Environment: effect of, 49, 69, 89-91;
    designing of, 92; of Church,
    symbols in, 109-10
Epistemology, 187
Ethics, 187
European cities, commerce in, 82-83
Evil: contrasting, with good, 27-28;
    symbols of, 106
Experience: strengthening, 11; role of,

in art, 14-15; primary, 35; enlarging, brings growth, 40
Expression, art as, 193

Family: identification experiences of, 36-39, 47; goals of, 49
Family home evening: held in tree, 37; held on mountain, 37-39
Fellowshipping, 121
Fish as Christian symbol, 105
Flowers: impact of, 43-44; in home and car of Dutch people, 45-46; in Church buildings, 118
"Form follows function," 52
Foyers, clutter in, 116
France, aesthetic training in, 93-94
Friends, impact of, 107-9
Function: conflicts in, in adjoining areas, 97; remembering, in designing buildings, 142-44
Future, cornerstones of, 196

Gifts, homemade, boy presents to family, 66
God's Own Junkyard, 96
Grow, Henry, 139
Grow, Stewart, 137
Growth, 33-34; experience enhances capacity for, 40; effect of environment on, 49; comes with struggling, 203

Heidegger, Martin, 193-94
High school art class, 16-19
Highways, design of, 90
Hogarthian line, 18
Home: spirit of, 48-49; designing, to meet changing needs, 49-50; placing of objects in, 57; poor design of, 59-61
Honolulu, neighborhood bomb shelter in, 85-86

Hooks of identification, creating, 34-39
Hospital, military, despair evident in, 4-6
Hotel room, sacrament meeting held in, 115-16
Hymns, singing of, family fathers for, 66

Idealism, 187-89
Identification: creating hooks of, 34-39, 126-27; with good things, 40-41; points of, in community, 81-82; links of, with Church, 125-26
Imagination, 149-50
Impressionist painters, 57
Infants, study of, with mothers, 49
Involvement in art, 148

Japanese examples of spirit, 42-43
Jesus Christ, xii
Joy through sensitivity, xii
Judgment of art, 190

Kant, Immanuel, 189-91
Keller, Helen, 5-6, 197
Kimball, Spencer W., 62, 75-76
Kline, Franz, 168-70

Lamb as symbol of Christ, 104
Language of spirit, 24
Lessing, 203
Lewis, friend who died in airplane crash, 107-11
Light of Christ, 29
Lindbergh, Charles, 150
Lions, symbolism of, 103-4
Litter, visual, 50, 56-57, 61-62; in the community, 71-72; combatting against, 73-75
Logic, 187

Lowenfeld, Viktor, 77-78

Makeup, teenage girl applying, 129
Malls, shopping, 83
McKay, David O., xiii
Mediocrity: too many accept, 76; spirit cannot survive on, 195
Mental illness, 90
Metaphysics, 187
Michelangelo, 167-68, 188
Milton, John, 184
Modern artists, 168-72
Monuments, 94-95
Morality, connection of art with, 192-93
Mosaic, children create, for school, 127
"Moses," by Michelangelo, 167-68
Music: visual, 18-20; playing of, during sacrament, 113-14; expressing, with crayons and paper, 146-48

Neutra, Richard, 69-71, 90-91, 97-88
Noah, xii
Nuclear energy, reservoirs for, 182-83

One-hundred-year-old woman, shaking hands with, 133-34
Opposition in all things, 21, 27-28
Organ: music of, 113-14; in Salt Lake Tabernacle, 140
Organic art, 61
Organic design, 96, 142
Oriental countries, examples of spirit in, 42-43

Paint-by-number kits, 15
Paintings: meaning of, vs. existence of, 189; of quality, acquiring, 191
Paper wad, artistic lines in, 17-18
Parables, Jesus provided identifications through, 40
Parents, responsibility of, to teach sensitivity, 16, 28-29

Paris, chapel built in, 126-27
Park, neighbors join in building, 86-88
Paul, 200
Pearl Harbor, 81, 85
"Peasant's Boots, The," 194
Pencil pilots, 149
Philosophy, 186-87; personal, developing, 199
Pioneers: appreciating, 134; arrival of, in Salt Lake valley, 135
Plant, spirit imparted to room by, 43
Plato, 188
Polio, girl with, spiritual strength of, 198
Pollock, Jackson, 170-72
Pollution, combatting against, 73
Pornography, "redeeming values" of, 25
Primary experience, 35
Prince Albert, 93
Prison, experiment in, 98-99
Progression, eternal principal of, 203-4

Quillen, I. James, 69

Religion, connection of aesthetics with, 188
Rembrandt van Rijn, 172-77
Reservoirs of spirit, 182-84
Ridges, Joseph, 140
Rock gardens, 64-66
Rockerfeller, Laurance S., 92
Rocking chair, sculpture of boy in, 151-52
Rotterdam, rebuilding of, 88-89
Rush hour, 83-85

Sacrament, sensitive partaking of, 121-22
Sacrament meeting: distractions in, 114-15; held in hotel room, 115-16
Salt Lake Tabernacle. See Tabernacle
Salt/pepper/sugar set, 54-56
Santa Clauses, identical, 13

Satan, plan of, 203
Schiller, Friedrich, 192-93
School buildings, sensitive design of, 70-71
Sculpture: simple test for, 95; by Dennis Smith, 151-62; girl weeps at beauty of, 201
Searching, importance of, 203-4
Second mile, going, 197
Selander, Alma, 113
Self-interest, sacrificing, for public good, 98
Self-portraits by Rembrandt, 176-77
Sensitivity: vision is born of, xi-xii; need for, xiii; search for, unexpected rewards in, 3; parents' responsibility to teach, 16; selecting companions who possess, 27
Singh, Sadhu Sundar, 22-23, 198
Slashes of spirit, 170
Smith, Dennis, 148, 151-62
Smith, Joseph, 97-98
Smith, Joseph Fielding, 110-11
Smith, Lewis, 107-11
Socrates, 187
Souvenirs, poor design in, 51
Spirit: various dimensions of, xi, 121; reawakening of, in disabled veterans, 6-7; gift of, 23, 66; definition of, 23-24; language of, 24; destruction of, by worldly ideas, 24-25; different columns of, 26-27; definition of, includes *energy*, 40; of home, 48-49; of community, 98; different parts of, complement each other, 121; stimulation of, by the arts, 146; gives life and energy, 181; reservoirs of, 182-84; is essence of every activity, 196; eternal nature of, 197
"Spirit stick," 46
Squaw Peak, 37-39
Steeples, symbolism of, 124
Stereotyped activities, dangers of, 13

Storm: men lost in, 22-23; car stalled in, Dutch people help with, 45-46
Study, the Lord urges, 27
Submarine, imaginary, sculpture of, 155-56
Sullivan, Louis, 52
"Supper at Emmaus," by Rembrandt, 175-76
Survival Through Design, 90
Symbols, 103; lions as, 103-4; Christian, 104-6; power of, 106; as spiritual link to abstract concepts, 106-7; of Church environment, 109-10; steeples as, 124

Tabernacle, Salt Lake: masterful design of, 134; background surrounding construction of, 135-40; unique acoustics of, 141; "organic design" of, 142-44; spirit of, 145
Tabernacle In the Desert, A, 137
Table, identifying with, 34-35
Tanner, Virginia, dance classes of, 15-16
Taste: lack of, 92-94; improving, of Church members, 95
Teenage girl applying makeup, 129
Telephone poles, 61-62
Testimony, identification is tool in gaining, 40
Thought, design in, 186; six major areas of, 187
Tibet, men lost in storm in, 22-23
Tokonoma, Japanese alcove of beauty, 42-43
Trailer: painting, 36; flowers on table, 43-45
Trash: family living amidst, 62; dollars spent to remove, 96
Trees: children's drawings of, 14; Van Gogh's struggle to paint, 164-65; studying paintings of, 165; observing, in nature, 166-67
Tricks, artistic, 10-11, 15

Trophies, displaying, in church building, 116-18
Truth, search for, 203
Turkey, child's drawings of, 8-13
Turkish cities, statues in, 94

Van Gogh, Theo, 164
Van Gogh, Vincent, 163-65, 194
Veterans, disabled, Helen Keller speaks to, 5-6
Vision, spiritual: importance of, xi; effects of, on perception, xii
Visual music, 18-20

Warsaw, rebuilding of, 89
Washington, D.C., group marching on, 75
Water, irresistibility of, 156
Woman, one-hundred-year-old, 133-34
World, challenges of, 24-25
World's Fair, 93
Wright, Frank Lloyd, 61, 142

Young, Brigham, 98; envisions Tabernacle, 136-37

Zoning ordinances, 97